The Art of Why

The Art of Why

Steve Luckenbach

ISBN: 1507807449
ISBN 13: 9781507807446

What people are saying about Steve Luckenbach and *The Art of Why:*

"Steve Luckenbach is more passionate and alive than anyone I have met. His book should come with a warning: 'This message will be hazardous to the ordinary life.' It is a must read for anyone who wants more out of life."

—Dr. Kevin Elko, Corporate and NFL Consultant and author of *The Pep Talk*

If you've ever had a three-year-old, you've probably been driven to distraction by being peppered with the question, "WHY?" If you relent, you will often end up both down a rabbit hole of answers and be filled with frustration. Steve is no three-year-old, he'll get you thinking about "WHY?" in a positive, witty way. For example, one of the things The Art of WHY will teach you is the happiness benefit of gratitude, and in the end, you'll be grateful for Steve's influence on your life through his book.

—Roger Hall, Ph.D., Business Psychologist, Compass Consultation, Ltd.

"As a consultant in my previous life, and as a University President, I have hired and watched hundreds, perhaps even thousands of speakers, coaches, and consultants. There are those who rely on sheer enthusiasm, and those with a more cerebral approach. Steve Luckenbach is one of the rare talents capable of effectively applying both. His presentations are thoughtful and thought provoking, instructional and enlightening, and passionate and motivating. He pulls no punches in shining the light on both successes and failures - not only for the industry, but himself as well. He is a guy who walks the talk and has achieved the success he wants others to share. For those who can't get to one of Steve's presentations, this book serves as the next best thing."

---Greg Salsbury, Ph.D., President, Western State Colorado University, Author of *Retirementolgy: Rethinking the American Dream in a New Economy*

Many thanks to those who have given me the opportunity to speak. Their support and the encouragement from their attendees have brought this second book to life.

This book is dedicated to my children, Gavin, Gabrielle and Grayson, for their never-ending love, inspiration and belief in me.

Table of Contents

Introduction

My Country, 'Tis a Mess

"From my earliest years there was something else going on inside me than vague aspirations to make a name for myself and a stir in the world; something that led me to feel myself a stranger among strangers in a strange land, whose true habitat was elsewhere; that brought an indefinable melancholy into my life, especially in its early years, and, at the same time, a mysterious exaltation, an awareness that, mixed up with the devices and desires of the ego, there were other possibilities and prospects, another destiny whose realization would swallow up time into Eternity, transform flesh into spirit, knowledge into faith and reveal in transcendental terms what our earthly life truly signifies."

—MALCOLM MUGGERIDGE, CONVERSION: THE SPIRITUAL JOURNEY OF A TWENTIETH-CENTURY PILGRIM

As I sit down to write this, I have been in my industry, the financial services industry, for 25 years. When I joined my company, Jackson National Life Insurance Company, in January 1996, we had just $748,000 in variable annuity sales at the end of 1995. By year-end of 2013, Jackson's variable annuity sales were well over $20 billion.1 While these sales numbers illustrate tremendous growth, I would suggest the true measure of Jackson's success is NOT in our sales numbers.

It's that we've remained true to our purpose. What's interesting is not what we accomplished, but *why* we accomplished it. Instead of pursuing the fast buck by giving people everything they want the second they wanted it, we said, "No. We are going to serve, not sell." Most people in my industry are focused not on why, but on *what* and *how*. What to do and how to do it. What to sell and how to sell it. I believe the reason my company has grown, even during the financial turmoil that has gripped the United States since 2008, is because we are all about *why*.

My industry is emblematic of the condition of our entire culture. We are a nation gripped by endless questions and doubts about *what* and *how*. What should I do for a living? How can I make more money? What do I need to buy to be seen as more prosperous than my neighbor? How do I avoid bankruptcy? Some of these are important questions, but I would suggest that they bypass the core question of our times, which is to ask *why*.

Philosopher Friedrich Nietzsche said, "He who has a why to live, can bear almost any how." Yet we evade questions of why in our culture. I think that's because asking why forces us to confront our choices and, in the past 20 years, we don't exactly have a track record of stellar choices! Political gridlock, ignoring climate change, a culture of unlimited greed, piling up mountains of government and personal debt...shall I go on? When we focus on what and how, we keep our noses to the grindstone, intent on making money and buying what we want. When the *what* is more, we can also easily justify the *how* of more debt to get it. We don't look up or around, so we're spared the agony of assessing our motivations and asking, "Why did I do that?"

WITHOUT WHY, WE'RE LOST

Not asking why is comforting in the short term. Nobody benefits from being bludgeoned with poor choices. But in the long term, we're lost if we can't face the *why* of the choices we are making. Each of us is a blend of science and art. Science is grounded in observation and theory, hard facts and empirical evidence: share prices and crop reports, cholesterol counts and final scores. That's essential; we need hard facts and scientific thinking to make sense of the world on a daily basis. Science is about what and how. It doesn't concern itself with meaning. Why is not in the vocabulary of the geneticist or botanist.

But we're also artists. We're creatures of intuition and creative vision. Those are not based on empirical facts (you can't quantify the moment when Steve Jobs had the inspiration for the iPhone), but they are no less important than the what and how of science. The key is that expressing our artistic selves means that we must have the courage to ask the question *why*:

- Why does this technology not work as well as it should?
- Why must I purchase things because my friends have them?
- Why have I put on 40 pounds in the last ten years?
- Why am I unhappy?

Looking at those questions, it's not hard to see why we duck and dodge *why*. Those are hard questions. They put us on the spot. They pin us down and leave us no escape from ourselves. They demand accountability and, my friends, accountability is something we've become extraordinarily good at avoiding in the United States of America.

CANCER OF THE ACCOUNTABILITY

Set aside your politics for a few minutes and look at the actions we've taken as a nation. We have created an economy of speculation built on a house of cards made up of unprecedented personal and government debt, unsustainable entitlement programs, and gross inequity between rich and poor. We have fought wars of questionable value that became quagmires, making us little safer while costing us thousands of lives and trillions of dollars. We have built suburbs and exurbs in regions such as the Southwest that are susceptible to periods of high rainfalls, as well as extreme drought cycles.[2]

Those were all decisions made by human beings, and they represent the worst of *what* and *how* thinking: How can we get rich quick without spending years building something? What can we do to expand our military power? What will give us a short-term rush of pleasure? How can we turn the Sun Belt into billions in profit? Never a question about *why* we did these things. That would demand accountability. It would force us to look in the mirror and see a people that have become broke, fat, divided and on the ledge of catastrophe...*and we are responsible!*

This terminal lack of accountability has our nation in crisis. Read the discourse online or listen to our talk radio: it's always someone else's fault. If it's not the liberals, it's the conservatives. If it's not the gays, it's the Muslims. If it's not the unions, it's the corporations. Anything we can do to dodge our own culpability in what's gone wrong, we do. That's better than the alternative: standing before the mirror, looking at our flabby reflection in a torn "America, love it or leave it" t-shirt, facing our failures and our misguided decisions. That's painful. It's frightening. We'd rather not, thank you.

RUNNING FROM MY FATHER

The trouble with avoiding the question *why* is that it imprisons us. If financial advisors don't ask why they are in business, they'll always be pushing products on customers who will up and leave them as soon as somebody else has a better product. If we as a people don't have the courage to ask *why*, then we're trapped in a cycle of endless consumption, collapse, recovery and repeat. This is not the recipe for a thriving civilization.

But if we can start asking that toughest of questions and embracing the answers, then we become free. We learn to value the intangible as much as the tangible. We build our lives around the tangible—cars, money, houses and beyond. I did the same thing earlier in my career; I based my self-esteem on the acquisition of more. The more I had, the more I was worth, or so I told myself. The trouble is that nothing in this life is free, dear reader. Everything in life comes at a price, and that price is usually in the form of time spent away from the people and pursuits that truly matter to us.

I built a life on acquiring the tangible and it very nearly cost me my marriage. I barely escaped when I, with great effort and help from my wife, began to ask the question *why*. Why did I believe that I had to grasp for more and more to the demolition of all that I should be holding dear? The answer was that I was trying to prove that I was better than my father, who had abandoned me when I was eleven years old. More on that later.

The point is that once I understood *why*, I was free. Instead of mindlessly chasing the tangible, I was able to *mindfully* change my behavior. I became accountable for my decisions and that gave me control over my future. I began recreating my life around the intangibles, the only things that last: my relationships with my wife, my children, and my friends, my work in my community, and my own spiritual health. That is why I have hope for this country, and for you.

LEARNED OPTIMISM

This country labors in a state of fear because we have based our entire existences—our personal senses of our own value—on that which, by definition, is impermanent and lies out of our control. The economy is a living thing and when it tumbles, it takes rich and poor alike with it. So we live in terror and stay awake nights worrying about what we might lose—expecting, in fact, to lose it. We exist in a state of what the psychologists Martin Seligman and Steven Maier called "learned helplessness."[3]

We see every setback through this prism:[4]

- Personal—It's my fault.
- Pervasive—It's going to undermine every aspect of my life.
- Permanent—Things will never change.

The terrible truth about living for things based on what and how is that we set ourselves up to fear—and then we expect that fear to manifest. It's insane! If your entire sense of self is based on what you earn and what you own, then you're going to be riddled with bullet holes. Inevitably, you will lose money when you sell a house. You'll lose out on the promotion. Your neighbor's Bentley will outshine your Lexus. It's a fact. If all that matters is what you have and how you get it, then two truths will dominate your life:

1. You will do anything to continue getting more of what defines you.
2. It will never be enough and you'll live in terror of losing it.

As a people, we need a shot of Seligman's "learned optimism."[5] When people base their self-worth on that which cannot be taken away, they view life's bumps a little differently. Here's what I took from Seligman's work:

- Impersonal[6]—Sometimes, things just don't work out.
- Isolated[5]—One mistake doesn't affect the rest of my life.
- Impermanent[5]—Things will be better next time.

That's *empowering*. Do you see how hard it is to think with a mindful sense of optimism when you're living in fear about failing at *what* and *how*? When we get past all that to ask *why*, we discover our purpose in life and the things that are meaningful to us. We can then begin serving those things rather than constantly chasing more.

Don't get me wrong. This is not a screed against capitalism or earning a great living, not at all. However, it is a passionate plea to understand not only what makes you successful, but also what *constitutes* success. Success is most emphatically *not* having the biggest house you can afford or selling out your values to make a killing on Wall Street. It's knowing that each day, you are serving the people and the purpose that holds the greatest meaning for you in the best, most honest, most generous way possible. It's knowing that if you lost everything tomorrow but your name, you would still be rich because you would have your honor, pride, ethics, and people who love and respect you.

The Art of Why is an idealistic book. But this is a time when idealism, not ideology, is sorely needed. It's a book about hope, asking painful questions, and finding the courage to be accountable for the answers. Even if you feel that you are proceeding through life on a steady course with fair winds and calm seas, it's still worth looking at *why* from time to time, because we can all lose our way. Fortunately, we can all know how to find it again.

I hope this book will be your map.

Steve Luckenbach
August 2012

Chapter 1

Know Your Why

"The way you get meaning into your life is to devote yourself to loving others, devote yourself to your community around you, and devote yourself to creating something that gives you purpose and meaning."

—MITCH ALBOM, AUTHOR OF *TUESDAYS WITH MORRIE*

Jim Rohn, the world-class speaker and trainer, said, "When the why becomes powerful, the how becomes easy." The book *Start with Why* by Simon Sinek, which is a gift to our nation, encapsulates that idea beautifully. Read this book. In it, Sinek addresses the tendency for people to chase the tangible and, in the process, surrender all that makes them who they are.[7] He writes, "People don't buy what you do, they buy why you do it."

What does that mean? Here's a personal example: The writer who helped me put together both of my books came to my attention because of a financial advisor out of Little Rock, Arkansas, named Rob Holdford. He had helped Rob write a wonderful book called *LIFEonomics*, which is about living free of worry and regret. But what made Rob recommend my co-author to me wasn't his skill with the written word; plenty of people can write. No, what made Rob recommend this fellow to me with such passion was *why* he had helped

Rob write his book. He believed in the material. He wanted to help people. He wanted to share his own wisdom while enhancing Rob's. If he'd just done it for the paycheck, that connection would not have been there. No one would have been inspired.

HOW THE MIGHTY FALL

Knowing why you do what you do—and understanding how that awareness can change your behavior—is the key to escaping from this endless cycle: gain, fear of loss, actual loss and the sacrifice of principles to regain what's been lost. Self-awareness is all-important.

That's the cornerstone of one of the most important books I've read in recent years, *How the Mighty Fall* by Jim Collins, author of the bestselling *Good to Great*. In this book, Collins and his team of researchers examine the reasons that previously high-flying companies suffer an eventual collapse. He identifies five stages of the progression that leads from lasting success to dissolution:[8]

1. Hubris born of success—Unjustified arrogance and a sense that the rules that apply to everyone else don't apply to you.
2. Undisciplined pursuit of more—Abandoning the principles and ethics that helped you get to the top in order to chase after greater and greater profit for its own sake.
3. Denial of peril and risk—You can't see the danger to your character and future because you're blinded by your pursuit of more.
4. Grasping for salvation—You finally clue into your own decline but too late, and start taking desperate steps to save yourself.
5. Capitulation to irrelevance or death—You are finally forced to surrender to the reality that your pursuits have been empty and destructive, or you lose everything.

In creating this model, Collins was trying to track the downfall of corporations that lost their purpose for being and destroyed themselves by virtue of mindlessly chasing greater and greater profits at the expense of everything else. But this model also applies to individuals, and that is where the concept of "knowing your why" comes into play.

Each of us is subject to this same dynamic: rise to a certain level, get a taste of the "good life" that lies at the end of the rainbow, sell out more and more of our principles over time in order to get more and more of the rewards, then lose everything because those principles were what got us there. This fall is made far worse because of what we often lose during the long fall back to earth: our wealth, our family relationships, our freedom (in cases where we break the law) and once in a while, our very lives.

Why do we ride this roller coaster despite having a clear blueprint that points to inevitable failure and downfall? Because we're human. We don't learn easily. Each of us is wired with—and the more gifted and intelligent you are, the more this is hard-wired into you—a sense that somehow, we're different. We won't make the same mistakes as those *other* people, as Bud Fox in the film *Wall Street*. If you know someone who has ever had a substance abuse problem and heard them insist, "I can handle it," then you'll recognize the same thinking in a person—even in yourself—who presumes that they will be the one immune to the temptations of more money, more property and higher status.

But nobody is naturally immune. We build up our immunity to the abandonment of self for the pursuit of more the same way we build up our immunity to disease: inoculation. Only, instead of inoculating ourselves with a version of a flu virus, we inoculate by coming to understand why we do what we do. When you know the reason for your behavior—or see clearly that there is no reason—you can steel your resistance against those things that would drag you down, tear apart your family and turn you into someone corrupt and lost.

A good example of the danger here can be found in the story of Rick Tabish.[9] A hard-working man from a good Montana family, Tabish took his multiple trucking and hauling businesses to Las Vegas and he had a reputation for pushing the limits of the law. Today he admits that while the life he was leading left him feeling empty inside, he couldn't seem to stop…that is, until his friend, disgraced casino heir Ted Binion, died of an apparent drug overdose.

Tabish's unsavory associations soon led to his being arrested on a trumped-up murder charge, convicted, and spending ten years in prison. The story was the subject of four books as well as a TV movie, *Sex and Lies in Sin City*. Today, Tabish admits that he's wiser, and that he lost sight of what was really important in life. But that doesn't give him back a decade spent behind bars, nor does it restore his businesses or relationship with his children.

That's a classic example of rising to a certain height, casting off your values like so much ballast in order to rise higher, and falling hard while losing everything. It shouldn't take such brutal lessons for us to learn to ask why we do what we do—and more importantly, to *listen* to the answers. But often it does. So are we doomed to make awful, wrenching mistakes in judgment before we can absorb life's most important lessons?

BRUTAL FACTS

Simply put, no. As I said, we can and sometimes do get our lessons before we crash to earth. We inoculate ourselves against loss and irrelevance by accepting responsibility for our choices early on and understanding the *why* that lies behind all we will do in the future.

That understanding is everything. A man who embraces *why* he works long hours at his bank—because he wants to provide a secure life for his children and be a good dad—is far less likely to dive headfirst into greed and corruption than someone who mindlessly chases bonuses, cars and corner offices, heedless of what he's giving up to get them. In the long run, who do you think is happier, the man with a nice nest egg and kids who love him, or the rich guy with the broken marriage, whose kids barely know him?

The critical step here is finding your why *before circumstances give you no choice.* But it's not easy. There are many reasons that we have a hard time looking in that internal mirror and facing the truth about why we've made the choices we've made:

- Ego—we think we're the only people not vulnerable to corruption
- Weak self-esteem that makes even the slightest failure unacceptable
- Blame for others—it's always somebody else's fault
- Fear of taking responsibility for our results

Removing our blinders, dropping our self-delusions and looking with courage and clarity at our choices…it's hard. It can be agonizing. We are our own worst critics. We have trouble forgiving ourselves for our errors in judgment or our mislaid priorities. It's much more comfortable to drape a cover over that mirror like we're a Victorian home in mourning, ignoring those nagging interior voices and pressing on with what we're doing.

But there's a flaw in that logic (if you can even call it logic). Eventually, our choices catch up with us. Life bats last. You've seen the stories play out with the rich and famous: celebrity rises high and fast, turns his back on family and friends and good values in favor of the posse, the bling and the party life, and winds up falling hard and fast into obscurity, addiction, poverty or worse. Think Britney Spears. Think Tiger Woods. If it could happen to them, believe me, it can happen to you.

As Jim Collins knew and wrote in *Good to Great*,[10] sustainable success comes through disciplined thought and disciplined action. He wrote, "disciplined action without disciplined thought is a recipe for disaster." That's why, as you strive to align yourself with your *why*, it's so critical to face the truth of your life so far, so you can *change your thinking*.

One of my favorite quotes on this is a real eye- and mind-opener. It's from Brian Moran, the brilliant founder of a company called Strategic Breakthroughs:

> **"If you change an action without changing
> the thinking, you are incongruent,
> and human beings do not stay in
> a state of incongruence."**

For instance, you've probably heard personal trainers and fitness experts advise you to "think like a thin person." They're not suggesting that you can think the flab off your middle (but wouldn't that be cool?). What they are saying is that unless you change the thought processes that led to poor eating habits or a life sitting on the couch, any changes in behavior you make will only be temporary. That's why diets don't work; they don't demand a permanent change in thinking.

When your thoughts and actions are incongruent, actions won't sustain. You'll wind up pulling back toward your old thought patterns like a car with bad alignment pulling to one side.

How does one go about changing thoughts? In his book, Collins pointed out that the companies most likely to be great were those that were able to face the "brutal facts" of their industries. In other words, they set aside ego, corporate back-slapping, self-delusion and their need for control, and said, "Why are we in business? Why do our clients need us? What are we not doing well, what are our weaknesses, and how can we become better and stronger?" Then they set about getting better and stronger.

You cannot know your *why* and change your thinking until you can face the brutal facts about yourself. Brutal facts are those harsh truths about your past choices that you're not eager to revisit. Have you chased career growth at the expense of family? Have you let health slip to the point where you're having medical problems? Have you spent yourself into deep debt buying expensive junk you don't even want anymore?

Once you face up to your choices and their consequences, accept responsibility for their effects on your life, and understand why you made those choices, you'll be able to change your way of thinking. It's like cracking a safe that suddenly springs open; limitless wealth is there for the taking. It's like a light comes on and you say, "Of course! That's why I did that! I get it now!" When you deal with the pain and regret and get that self-knowledge, it's impossible to go back to the way you were.

WHO ARE YOU BEING?

In his marvelous book *From Selling to Serving*,[11] Lou Cassara writes, "Who you are being is far more important than what you are doing." If you remember nothing else from this book, remember that phrase. But what does it mean? Well, in my understanding, it means that the character and values you are expressing through your actions—and the impact those character and values have on other people—determine more about your long-term success than getting a certain promotion or making a specific investment.

Unfortunately, when we're not in touch with the *why* of what we do on a daily basis, we have little chance of being the kind of person that we would like to be. At best, we throw a few bones to the idealized version of ourselves, relying on our own inner press agent to make us look good to ourselves. That's why you find the CEOs of companies that dump toxic waste into the waterways also making big donations to environmental causes; it's great internal PR. But it's a lie. If the thinking doesn't change, the behavior doesn't change. Tokens are meaningless.

When you face your brutal truths and discover why you do what you do, you get in touch with who you should be on a daily basis. This is often a shock, because at one time or another, each of us has in his or her mind an idealized version of the person he or she wants to become. Inevitably, we're prosperous and healthy, but we're also noble and respected and happy. When we take a close look at the compromises we've made over the years, it can be jarring. It's not uncommon to realize with horror that we've sold out who we wanted to *be* in favor of what we wanted to *do* and *have*.

But horror soon turns to self-awareness and hope. We see that by facing up to how we've lost our way, we gain the power to find it again. Understanding why we make choices and take actions gives us the ability to make adjustments and recapture the spirit of that person we once intended to be.

This is the essence of the midlife crisis! You begin in your 20s filled with idealism and purpose and passion. You are going to shake the pillars of Heaven, change the world, and never, ever give in to The Man. Then, as the years go by you make one small compromise after another. Eventually they achieve critical mass, helped along by the pressures of family, kids, a mortgage, retirement savings, consumer culture, and so on. Twenty-five years after you swore you'd never give in to The Man, you *are* The Man! Men in particular, who because we cannot have children often define ourselves by what we do and what we earn, are especially vulnerable to this kind of midlife soul-searching.

I think it's healthy. Not that you should run off and have an affair in your newly bought Ferrari, but it's beneficial to get a mid-course correction. It's hard and it can hurt, but it's precisely this kind of crisis period that makes us reevaluate *what* and *how* and rediscover *why*. Such a period saved my marriage and possibly my life. Having the courage to face up to your brutal facts, accept responsibility for your choices and rediscover that your *why* can do the same for you!

THE DELIBERATE EXISTENTIAL CRISIS

In my last book, *Don't Believe Everything You Think*, I wrote at length about "hacking the epiphany." The idea was that for people to undergo a real sea change in their beliefs or values, they generally need to experience an epiphany, a sudden revelation of great truth. But because epiphanies are not something you can just order up at will, you've got to "hack" the thing like you would a computer. As I said in that book, "If you want to get on the train, stand next to the tracks."

I believe that the very process of discovering your *why* is epiphany-inducing. Questioning the values and actions that got you where you are today can create the very crisis of self-interrogation and uncertainty that leads to real breakthroughs. It's as though you are a crew on one of the many home-remodeling shows on TV today, tearing down the old drywall of a house that's falling down and looking for the flaws at the core so you can fix them. Once you get past your hardened attitudes toward money and success, you start to see where your assumptions break down. And we make a lot of false assumptions based on wishful thinking and self-delusion:

- "More money will make me happy."
- "I'll make it up to my kids one of these days."
- "I'm not fat, I'm big boned."
- "I drink when I go out with the boss. I don't have a problem."
- "I deserve that car/big screen/vacation home."

Step back and you can see how empty a life based on these ideas is. It's when people realize that they are worshipping the God of More that they have their midlife crises. I'm a fan of crisis. Sometimes, it's the only way to expose the core of your thinking (like the rotten beams in a poorly-built house, to return to that metaphor). When you question the very basic assumptions and beliefs that drive you, you go into mental free fall. There's nothing to hold on to. You start questioning everything about who you are and why you do what you do. That's healthy.

The trick is to ask those questions—to induce what I call a "deliberate existential crisis" earlier rather than later. Over the years, the more you steer your life based on *what* and *how* rather than *why*, the more damage piles up, like a tumor growing in your life. If you have a colonoscopy every five years like you're supposed to, you probably catch the polyps early and bingo—a clean bill of health. But if you let it go and ignore the pain, you wind up with stage IV cancer and you're done. It doesn't take much looking to see a trail of broken marriages, shattered families, trashed finances and personal misery—like the trail of destruction that follows a tornado—following men and women who have waited too long to start asking the hard questions.

THE DEATH OF TRIBALISM

So start asking. Start looking at where you are and where you once intended to be. In the space between your past intentions and your present condition, you will find unanswered "why" questions. That's so important, I'm going to repeat it:

**In the space between your past intentions
and your present condition,
you will find unanswered "why" questions.**

Your job is to figure out what those questions are and start answering them without looking away from the answers, no matter how painful they might be. Some of the questions you might encounter:

- Why did I give up on my passion to pursue my profession?
- Why did I marry the person I chose to marry?
- Why have I set my goals aside?
- Why has money become so important to me?
- Why have I let my health slip?
- Why am I not happy?

Believe me, finding and then answering those questions can be debilitating at first. The experience can wear you out. It's difficult to face our failures—to face that we're just as vulnerable as everyone else to losing our way. But redemption lies in *rediscovering* that way.

Knowing "why you are" also shows you "who you are," and this also frees you from the armed camps that form when we defend our biases and ideas against those who dare to disagree. You become less defensive because you know that your motives are real and in alignment with who you want to be. This offers an escape from the tribalism that often infects our discourse. In the marvelous documentary *Flight from Death: The Quest for Immortality*, the filmmakers make the convincing argument that anger against those who disagree with our culture, religion or politics is actually a manifestation of our anxiety about our own mortality. Since culture is a construct intended to lend meaning to our limited lives, the filmmakers say, anything that devalues that culture is a threat.

When we are living incongruently with who we once thought we would be, we will lash out to defend our choices—even when we know that the criticism is justified. That's why so many people in our current political environment viciously defend our modern version of capitalism even though it can be horribly destructive. Inside, they're thinking, "If I sacrificed everything meaningful to gain this wealth and power, I can't possibly tolerate the idea that it all may have been a terrible mistake! That simply can't be!" The result is an angry denunciation of anyone who disagrees.

But that disagreement, that harsh truth, is what sets us free. It's the path to *why*. And that is the path to salvation. We can be confident in our new choices and new behaviors because we know they are aligned with the person we know we've always meant to become. The trick, then, is becoming that person. That's a new path.

Chapter 2

SCIENCE VS. ART

*"How often people speak of art and science as though they were
two entirely different things, with no interconnection...that is all
wrong. The true artist is quite rational as well as imaginative...
if he does not, his art suffers. The true scientist is quite imaginative
as well as rational, and sometimes leaps to solutions where reason
can follow only slowly; if he does not, his science suffers."*

—Isaac Asimov

As I said before, you are part artist, part scientist. Science has become something of the new religion in our culture, and to be sure it has brought us many incredible advances that have made life safer, healthier, and more prosperous. Yet at the same time, some of the most important things in our lives are intangible, not supportable by empirical evidence. Love, loyalty, honor...these are not scientific terms. We are, all of us, part art and part science, part logic and part philosophy. If you are seeking the truth of your own *why*, you won't find it without embracing both halves of yourself.

You're probably aware of the concept of the left brain and the right brain. In the simplistic version, the left brain is the seat of logic, mathematics, rational thought and linear thinking. It's the domain of accountants and engineers. The right brain drives our intuition, emotion, creativity and passion. It's dominant in artists, writers, and musicians. Or so goes the theory. As with many things, the reality is more complex.

Down the center line of the brain, connecting these two hemispheres, runs a dense bundle of nerve fibers called the corpus callosum[12]. This is the bridge between left brain and right brain—between the rational and the intuitive. Because both sides of our brains are interconnected and interdependent, we are all creatures of the left and right brains. One side may be dominant in many of us, but each of us is a blend of creative and logical, hard science and artistic vision.

We all have a unique gift to serve. All artists struggle with what and how, and because you have a gift that serves others, you struggle at times, too. But the answer does not lie in what and how. We have a preoccupation with what and how because they have taken us so far. They are scientific questions. How do we increase crop yields? What genome hides the key to cancer? How do we boost the speed of the Internet? What element will give us clean nuclear reactors? Those are vital, civilization-shaping questions that we must ask! Absolutely.

The trouble comes when we run up against areas of endeavor that don't yield absolute answers. As a species, we are deeply uncomfortable with uncertainty. What and how answers give us concrete information. That's science. But why questions take us into the realm of philosophy, the territory of Big Questions, where what you don't know is more important than what you know. Why am I on this earth? Why do I do what I do? Why does God permit evil acts? The list of impossible questions goes on and on, and if we're not at peace with inconclusive answers, we close our ears to them and stick with what and how.

THE SOCIAL ANIMAL

Why questions cause pain for our inner artist. We are acutely aware of that pain and have developed beliefs and behaviors to avoid it. The hardening of our hearts blocks our gifts from flowing outward to the people they were meant to serve. Make no mistake: beliefs that are not true will limit your capacity to live as you were meant to live, to receive love and to give love.

Part of your journey toward joy and purpose is learning to balance your inner scientist and your inner artist—to see them as two faces of the same being, so to speak. In doing so, it's important to begin by seeing the weaknesses in reductionist thinking. Reduction is the act of reducing a phenomenon to its smallest, simplest possible component or cause.

For example, many cognitive scientists today adhere to the theory that the human mind is nothing more than a collection of neural signals predetermined by the laws of physics. In this model, called *eliminative materialism*,[13] here's what I took from Paul Churchland's research on the topic, the mind and free will are illusions, and we're not really conscious beings. Instead, we just think we're conscious because of the illusion created by firing synapses and surging neurotransmitters. I see it as a bleak, nihilistic worldview, where there is no consciousness and no soul.

Thinking like this—reduction to the point of absurdity for the sake of scientific dogma—has helped fuel what writer Richard Dawkins calls militant atheism. Where we were once a deeply superstitious culture, now the pendulum has swung to the other extreme. Millions of Americans scorn religion and spirituality, declare believers to be idiots, and insist that they have infallible knowledge that the universe is meaningless and purposeless. It's reductionism turned religion.

What's missing is balance. Skeptical thinking is critical in a modern society, but so is the ability to embrace what one does not know—to be a philosopher as well as a scientist. In his brilliant book, author Albert-Laszlo Barabasi shares his insight about reductionism.[14] It was, he writes, the driving force behind much of the research that made the 20th century such a time of incredible change. Reductionism tells us that to comprehend nature, we must decipher the parts. Once we know how the parts fit together, we know the whole story. Right?

No. That's like saying that if you take 1,000 people about whom you know everything—their histories, psychological profiles, and so on—and put them together in an apartment building, you can predict every interaction. You can't. New dynamics *emerge* from the interaction of the parts and produce outcomes you can't possibly predict. These "emergent systems" are changing everything we thought we knew about society, human behavior, the brain and more.

Basically, emergent systems are more than the sum of their parts. They create new things and are great at passing down wisdom and traditions through generations.

We are emergent systems. The brain is an emergent system. Marriage is an emergent system. Cultures are emergent systems. Whenever you take multiple forces and bring them together, you create emergent properties that upset the order of things. That's the Arab Spring, mega churches, and Occupy Wall Street. The reality of emergence means that hard science must co-exist with the philosophy in all of us—because if we are emergent ourselves, then we are capable of completely changing direction and becoming something tomorrow that we were not yesterday. We have the ability to act in new ways and change the direction of our lives.

PREPARE AND RESPOND

Are you passionate about what you do? Is your heart in your work? The first five years I was with my company, we were all art. We were building something from scratch and we didn't have anything *but* our art, our passion and commitment. People knew our hearts and they responded to the truth of what we were selling, which was service.

In the last few years, as the nation's economic situation has become unstable and frightening, we have swung more toward science, more toward what we feel we can control. Emphasis on the word *feel*. We can control very little beyond two things:

1.   How we prepare for what happens.
2.   How we respond to what happens.

Beyond that, we're basically guessing. We like to think that a focus on the empirical and the individual parts gives us control over what happens, at least to a degree. But that's an illusion! Life is an emergent property. The chain of causation that you step into every time you get out of bed in the morning would blow your mind if you could see it graphed out on paper! The world is emergent, and in order to make some sense of the chaos, all we can do is prepare and be able to respond in a healthy, productive way to what happens.

Here's the problem: Science does not equip us to do either very well. Science is all about hypothesis, evidence and theory. It's about what we can *know*. But we can't live by what we know, because we don't know what's going to happen. If we can't admit that we don't know, we won't see the need to prepare. That's why some people don't have insurance; they can't handle the idea that they don't know what will happen tomorrow!

Without philosophy—without knowing our *why*—we can't respond to what happens in ways that protects what we have and helps us grow and learn. Response becomes reaction, because when we don't know our true character, we can't respond to life's ups and downs with anything but panic and anger.

Let's say that you owned an apartment building in Miami in the mid 2000s,[15] when condominium conversions were on the rise. You saw dollar signs and convinced yourself that your business model was foolproof: convert to condos, sell out in months, rake in the dough. Then the real estate market in south Florida collapses as it did in 2007. Condo conversions stop dead. Buildings sit vacant (including yours). Fortunes vanish overnight.

You could not have prevented this from occurring. The events remain immutable. But if your inner artist is strong enough to embrace the fact that you can't know what is going to happen, you can prepare. You are not as surprised in case the bottom falls out of the market. Also, because you are in touch with your values and your true value proposition (your value to others), you can hold on to your perspective through these events, learn from them, find new opportunities in them, and even discover a new purpose. That's better than ignoring reality in favor of a false sense of control, and then when you go broke, jumping off a ledge.

Your analysis (science) of what to fear is not your greatest asset, but your greatest preoccupation. Your questions of what and how will be more easily answered when you are preoccupied with *why*. *Why* is your unique artistic expression of your greatest asset. With nothing more than science, you will always find reasons for fear. With a fifty-fifty balance of art and science the reasons for your fear may still exist, but you will also find reasons within your character for faith and hope. Art is about knowing (without knowing why) that you can overcome, that you can grow, that love is what matters in the end.

To quote my favorite Chinese proverb, "once we tend the root, the tree as a whole will be healthy." Your *why* is your root. To tend it you need a mix of scientific thinking and artistic leaps of faith.

THE BRAIN BUG

If we were Vulcans, we'd all have pointy ears. Oh, and the world would be logical. But we're not Vulcans. We're illogical beings. One of the fundamental maxims of the networking world is represented in a quote by Robert Knakal, "People work with people they like." That's true. We want to associate with and give our business to people who are competent, but also confident—people who we feel love and care about us and treat us as more than transactions. That's reality.

In my profession, I have seen advisors with so many letters after their names that they can't fit them on their business cards but have few clients. I've also seen advisors who didn't even graduate from college who have huge practices. Why? Love. Passion. Connection. Art. We as a people respond to those with passion and purpose, and those are not scientific qualities! Those are right-brained, illogical qualities that neuroscientists claim don't even exist. But they are forces in our lives.

The thing is, we're all subject to the workings of the brain. This amazing organ, which weighs about three pounds, is the seat of our humanity and our civilization. It gives us the godlike ability to project ourselves backward in time to learn from past experiences and forward in time to predict and visualize where we'll be in the future. But it's also got some bugs in the software. One of these bugs goes back to what I said about us being uncomfortable with uncertainty.

Basically, the brain hates the unknowable, so when it's presented with a question, it automatically leaps to an answer. Most of the time, the answer is incorrect, but that doesn't matter to the brain. It's wired to seek certainty (we'll get more into the reasons why later). That's bad enough when we're dealing with basically empirical, scientific questions about, for example, when to sell a certain stock. It gets worse when we're dealing with artistic, philosophical questions where there's nothing concrete to hold onto.

Go ahead, ask yourself a tough, challenging, existential question and see what your mind does. Try something like, "Why do I pursue my career?" Even as you read those words, your brain was concocting an answer. But there are two types of answers when we're faced with philosophical questions: limiting answers and empowering answers. In my opinion, the brain's default setting is to leap at simple, limiting answers. Human beings are conclusion-drawing machines. We love to say, "Well, that's all wrapped up." We love to feel like we have the answers, even if they're the wrong answers.

So what was your reflexive answer to "Why do I pursue my career?" It was probably something pseudo-noble like, "I have to provide for my family." That's an answer programmed into you by family and society. That's a limiting answer because it defines you by what you do, not by who you are. The immediate answers that the brain throws out like darts in a pub are usually as inaccurate as those darts. The deeper answers require a mental process:

-   Recognize the quick answer as erroneous.
-   Seek for deeper answers.
-   Recognize that the truth rests on realities that are not scientific.

But because those deeper answers rest on *why*, they are empowering. If your deeper answer to "Why do I pursue my career" is something like, "Because I am interested in improving the human condition," then there is vast potential in that answer for future growth. You are defining yourself by who you are, not by what you do.

Do you see the dichotomy? If you define your value by what you do, do you stop having value when you're not doing it? Tough question. But if your value is not what you do but *who you are*, then your value to others and to yourself is always present because you can never stop being who you are. True, you might change who you are over the years. But that value proposition is far more powerful and enduring than value created only by degrees, education or certification.

Even answering, "I don't know" is great because you're admitting the lack of purpose in what you do, which is the first step to positive change.

BIGGER, BETTER, MORE

Your value to others and to the world is in who you are being, not in what you are doing. Early in life, we hear this line: "One day, you'll be somebody." This phrase implies that you're not somebody now. It puts everything on what you do. You're only as good as what you earn, what you own or what you make. But those things are transitory. We cannot find happiness by worshipping at the Church of Bigger, Better, More.

When we value what we do more than who we are, we can't sit still. When we believe that our greatest value is what we do, we fail to see the big picture. We fail to invest time in things that elevate us. *Why* matters because, without it, we forget to nurture the root (thinking) because we are preoccupied with the tree (action).

My parents divorced when I was 11 years old and my mom remarried a hard-working man who was a "human doing." I'll never forget a time when my sister, mom, stepdad and I were relaxing on a small houseboat, on a beautiful lake, on a beautiful day. Only my stepdad wasn't relaxing. He had a screwdriver in his hand and was scouring the boat to find screws to tighten. He was unable to just *be*; he had to be doing something! I love my stepdad but, ironically, the only loose screw was in his head!

How many people do you know who have forgotten the why of serving, purpose and meaning for the sake of chasing more stuff, more money, more success? How did those people turn out? Are they happy? Do they have great relationships with their kids? Do they wish they could go back and change things? Well, they can't. Let me share a harsh truth with you:

> **You are not the exception to the rule that living for more produces less.**

Living for more produces less. That's an axiom to live by. We tend to want what's measureable, what we can point to and say, "There! There's how well I've done in my life! I own six cars, I have a mansion and a vacation home and a condo in Vail and have you seen my bank balance?" That's great. I won't ever begrudge anyone his financial prosperity. But ask yourself, what is the point of making it if you don't keep it? The things that we chase, the measureable winnings that appeal to the left, rational, scientific side of our brain, *do not endure*. They come and they go. And if they come into your life with volatility and drama, they will exit your life the same way.

Throughout this book, I will share personal beliefs that I call Luckenbach Laws. Here's the first one, relevant to this idea:

> *The sustainability of your prosperity and happiness is in direct proportion to the sustainability of the emotions and mindset that bred that prosperity and happiness.*

Cause to pause? I think so.

Your ability to balance the scientific and artistic states of being—the calculating and the passionate—determines how well you'll hold on to what you build. All of us have a predisposition, or serving ego, for giving, serving and loving.[16] It's our nature. But when you suppress that nature in order to pursue more—when you betray your values, taint your character, ignore your children or break the law to rake in a few more bonuses, you veer far from those essential qualities. Is it any wonder that the Bernie Madoffs of the world are miserable failures in the end? Such people build their "success" on the worst human qualities: greed, deception, malice and envy. No person can sustain those emotions for long without breaking down. They destroy the person and what that person has built.

Success built on who you are and what you care about tends to be slower and less flashy—think a local merchant rather than Donald Trump—but it also tends to rest on a foundation of part art, part science. That's the success that lasts. It's a success that doesn't allow for short cuts. If you're going to build your career based on who you are, and part of who you are is a dedicated and loving parent, then part of your time is going to be spent with your kids…at a time when others in your field might be slaving away in their offices and missing piano recitals. In the short run, those people might have an edge over you. But life is a marathon, not a sprint. It's not about what you earn, but what you keep.

Chapter 3

HOW THE MIGHTY FALL

*"It is the mark of the mind untrained to take its own processes as
valid for all men, and its own judgments for absolute truth."*

— ALEISTER CROWLEY

I've already referenced the extraordinary book by Jim Collins, *How the Mighty Fall*.
While Collins wrote this book after three years of research to apply to corporations, it also applies perfectly to individuals. It tracks the predictable and totally avoidable path to downfall that people often follow when they become caught up in what and how—in money and power and success—and lose sight of *why*.

In this chapter, I'd like to take a closer look at the five stages of decline that Collins describes and dig into the heart of each to see how they relate to our discussion about knowing your *why*. To recap, these are the five stages of decline:

1. **Hubris born of success**
2. **Undisciplined pursuit of more**
3. **Denial of peril and risk**
4. **Grasping for salvation**
5. **Capitulation to irrelevance or death**

Put them together and I believe these five steps track the inexorable downward slide of individuals who become enamored of how and what at the expense of why. Of course, in becoming aware of these stages, you gain the ability to spot the danger signs in your own behavior and perhaps catch yourself before things become dire. What's dire? How about losing your marriage, going bankrupt, winding up in prison or dropping dead of a stress-induced heart attack? I think it's safe to say we'd all rather avoid those fates.

So let's have a look at how the mighty do, in fact, fall.

HUBRIS BORN OF SUCCESS

The Greek definition of hubris is "arrogance", which I interpret as hurting the innocent.[17] Other writers have defined it as usurping power that lies rightly with God. Victor Frankenstein, the namesake of the famous novel by Mary Shelley, was filled with hubris. He thought he could defy nature and restore life to the dead without any consequences. That arrogance proved to be his undoing. So really, this is the heart of Hubris Born of Success:

Arrogant thought and action with presumed impunity.

In other words, you're a badass. You kick butt and take names in business, finance, law, media, whatever. You've got a wallet a foot thick and an ego to match. You are so good, you tell yourself, that you're immune to consequences. The rules that apply to others don't apply to you. Dammit, you're above the rules!

I wish this was a caricature, but it's not. Look at fallen titans from the recent past and you see precisely this pattern. History is littered with people who, because they had some early success, decided that they were above the rules, above the law and above morality. This is the beginning of the slippery slope, and what makes it so dangerous is that it comes about while we're nearing the peak of our success! We're closing deals, getting praise, making money hand over fist, and our egos LOVE IT. We start to believe our own press clippings, as they say.

When this happens to an individual who has based his entire self-worth on what he does and how much he earns, the effects are devastating. Suddenly, with the achievement of more material success, his self-worth is validated in the most dramatic way possible. He has cars, homes, and a fat bank account—he MUST be a great person! Never mind that his kids don't care what he earns or how big his bonus is; they just want their daddy. But a person who enters into this first phase with a system of self-esteem that is already built around material achievements—someone totally preoccupied with what and how and with no interest in why—can *only* think in terms of the material achievements.

The greatest hazard of this stage—and why the slide downhill is so difficult to arrest after it begins—is that it feels so good. The person is probably not experiencing any real consequences. He's just getting rich and powerful and his self-esteem is booming. It's easy to see that someone not firmly anchored to a strong sense of *who he is being* can disappear into hubris and never resurface. If you don't already have a foundation of self-worth based on who you are and why you do things, (rather than what you earn and how much influence you have) it's going to be nearly impossible for you even to see the danger you're in.

Danger? Yes. The danger lies in that universal rule I mentioned before, which is that nothing is free. Or to put in another way:

Nobody is bigger than the game.

The reason those casinos in Las Vegas are so enormous is because the games, from roulette to blackjack to slots, are mathematically designed to give the house a slight advantage. Over time, unless you have phenomenal luck, the house will win. That's why big winners get comped rooms and all sorts of privileges designed to keep them gambling. The casinos know that eventually, if you play long enough, the odds will catch up with you. Under these circumstances, winners are not winners; they're just losers who don't know it yet.

I don't have to beat you over the head with that metaphor for it to be clear how it applies here. When you betray your values for the sake of success, it will always catch up with you in one way or another. You'll step beyond the bounds of the law and wind up wearing an orange jumpsuit. You'll neglect your family and suffer a ruinous divorce. You'll have a nervous breakdown. Or you'll suffer the slow corruption of loneliness, knowing that you sold out your principles for empty material gain that in the end means nothing. Again, I'm not against wealth. I am against wealth at the price of that which makes wealth worth having: companionship, children, friends, community, purpose, faith, love and peace of mind.

The house always wins in the end. But when you're firmly in the hubris phase, you won't see it. You think you're invincible. You think that just showing up means the streets run with rivers of gold. In your arrogance, thinking everything is coming easily, you sow the seeds of your own destruction.

For each of these five stages, I'll share some of the warning signs that I feel show you're at risk of sliding further down the slope...so you can save yourself. A few of the warning signs for this stage include the following:

- Lack of humility about what you do
- Scoffing at your competitors because they don't measure up to you
- Scorn for people who don't value what you value
- A willingness to suck up to those with power and influence, even if you can't stand them personally
- Gradually breaking more of the rules of conduct in your profession to gain an edge
- Lax preparation on the assumption that you can do no wrong
- Obsessively comparing your successes to those of others and measuring those successes only by a few tangibles such as sales made or dollars earned

In the world of financial services, it's easy to spot the advisors who are in this first stage. They swagger. It's all about them, not their clients. They push product in order to get commissions. That's it. There's little regard for purpose or mission, and anyone who suggests otherwise is a loser. Inevitably, these types are the first ones to go belly-up when the economy turns, but the problem is that they take a lot of people down with them.

UNDISCIPLINED PURSUIT OF MORE

You're the best. You know it, and you tell everybody about it. Now comes a scene right out of *Animal House*. Tom Hulce was in the dorm room with a drunk girl, and an angel appeared on one shoulder telling him to leave her alone, while a devil appeared on the other urging him to violate her. Well, when you get into stage two, you've got an angel on one shoulder and a devil on the other...only the devil is a lot bigger and louder.

This is where the slippery slope gets steeper and you pick up speed. Successes begin to breed successes and you begin to get a taste for the money and influence that you're generating. At some point, you begin to rationalize away your values. Break that longstanding personal prohibition on stealing someone else's idea? Heck, it won't hurt just this once! Fudge some numbers on a balance sheet? Come on, everybody does it! Like the main character in the Hans Christian Andersen story "The Garden of Paradise," every step you take toward temptation becomes easier and easier.

It's a Faustian bargain. If you don't *start* your climb to success with a firm grounding in the fundamental personal reasons why you are doing what you do, then it's quite easy to become drunk on the act of grabbing more and more rewards. Soon, you're cutting corners and betraying your formerly inviolable personal principles to close a deal or chase more profit. Eventually, you leave ethics, morals and even laws by the side of the road like so much baggage. The devilish part of all this is that it's occurring when you're at the peak of your "success" (I put that word in quotes for a reason). You're making big money, getting rich even, rolling with major players, getting your name in the trade press and being considered executive VP or even C-suite material. How could this be bad?

That's where the quotes come in. When you throw aside all your moral and ethical discipline (and maybe your physical and dietary discipline, too) to chase bigger and more, you stop knowing what success is. The undisciplined pursuit of more is the stage where you unknowingly cast aside all of the qualities (your ingenuity, work ethic and sincerity, for example) in order to get greater and greater rewards by any means possible. No cut is too short. The end justifies the means. The rules are for suckers.

Corporations that have done this are legendary...and not in a good way. Sadly, I could go on for a while. Of course, within the legal structure of the corporation are individuals making the decisions to chase profit at the expense of everything else, so these are individual failures as well. In the end, the undisciplined pursuit of more is tragic because the players don't even see that they are sowing the seeds of their own destruction by turning their backs on ethics, moderation, and the rules of law. As always, the rules don't apply to them.

This stage of the process highlights why it's so crucial to understand and accept your personal *why* before you venture into your career. That's your only protection against the seductions of money, power and fame. If family, honor, community and faith are the hallmarks of your success, then you are better able to resist the seductions that come along almost every day.

What are the signs that you're sliding down this slippery part of the slope? Here are a handful of major ones:

- You find yourself concocting complex rationalizations for your actions.
- Your family life is suffering from a lack of time investment.
- You obsess over your earnings and bonuses.
- You fudge numbers on everything from sales reports to expense reports and make excuses for it like "Everyone does it."
- You're spending more and more time with colleagues who are known as soulless sharks.
- You have more material wealth than ever but are more stressed than ever about keeping it.

Stress is born of fear. According to Tom Scheve, when we say we're stressed, we're really saying that we fear that we're not making the right choices. For instance, everyone has the exact same amount of time. It's what we choose to do with our time that determines whether we live well or poorly. In reality, "stress" is a socially acceptable term for refusing to ask the question, "What am I so afraid of?" It carries with it no ownership or accountability.

With ownership, you are empowered and required to address your fear. If you can't, you're in danger territory. Everything is telling you that you are doing well, riding the crest of the wave toward big riches and big dreams fulfilled. But if your compass of success only points in the direction of what and how, you're actually headed for a major wipeout.

DENIAL OF PERIL AND RISK

In 2010, court investigators found that (for an unnamed company) executives regularly used accounting tricks (such as a repurchase agreement that temporarily removed undervalued securities from the company's balance sheet) at the end of each quarter to make its finances appear stronger than they actually were. But even as the company's positions in worthless, subprime mortgage-backed securities were eroding its ability to remain viable, its executives were claiming that the company was in solid shape to stage a recovery.

It wasn't true. In September 2008, the NYSE delisted the company, which eventually went bankrupt.

What happened? In part, the people who ran this company systematically denied the peril and risk of the situation they had created. They did everything they could do to cover it up and pretend it wasn't happening. Why? Because after enough time in the self-created reality of pursuing more at all costs, it's easy to believe that reality bends to your will. But that isn't the case. Reality always snaps back into a rigid enforcement of the basic rules, and the more egregious your violation of those rules, the more that snap-back hurts. The snap-back to reality killed this company.

Denial of peril and risk entails deep self-delusion—clinging to the idea that one is untouchable and that even the most obvious red flags of coming disaster are meaningless. This is a self-deceptive state of mind that almost inevitably leads to panic. The typical progression goes something like this:

-   Early signs of trouble, such as big financial losses or a separation from your spouse
-   Refusal to see the signs for what they are, and sometimes the self-created belief that people who don't see things your way are enemies
-   More serious signs of trouble, such as a legal investigation
-   Desperate, futile attempts to cover up or patch the problematic events
-   Blaming
-   Panicked actions to hide wrongdoing or repair damage that's already beyond repair

But most often, this stage manifests by people doing...nothing. They continue business as usual, carrying out the grossest violations of the principles they once held dear because the relentless pursuit of more has recalibrated their sense of self-worth. Once upon a time, they may have seen themselves first as spouses, parents or pillars of the community. But now, self-love is all about how much and how big. The needy, greedy ego simply won't accept the notion that the actions that built it up to be so big and healthy could have been misguided. So it says, "No."

The result is complete denial of even the possibility that one's choices could be ill-considered or destructive—or that they should even be questioned. By this time, the person harboring this attitude is ripe for a fall. The signs that you are at this stage of this process:

- Feelings of foreboding and doom
- A massive increase in personal stress
- Increasingly panicked activities designed to prop up financial gains to peak levels
- Initial signs of damage to your empire
- More principled friends and associates washing their hands of you
- Scapegoating

In his brilliant book *Capitalism Hits the Fan*,[18] economist Richard Wolff says that one of the reasons that the Great Recession has been so devastating is that the American consumer used debt to maintain a standard of living that was no longer viable. After decades of labor shortages, the 1980s brought the devastating one-two-three-four punch of automation, job offshoring, and more women in the workforce and massive immigration, claims Wolff. The resulting labor glut led to lower wages, the decline of union jobs and, for the first time in recent memory, a generation likely to be worse off than its parents' generation. In denial of this new reality, says Wolff, Americans turned to credit cards and home equity lines to acquire more material possessions and create the illusion of a higher standard of living. When the collapse of the real estate market destroyed that illusion, denial became disaster.

That's the mindset that afflicts people in the Denial of Peril and Risk stage. It's a time when the desperate need to preserve the toxic state of more justifies the most corrupt actions and the most startling mental gymnastics. All are doomed to failure.

GRASPING FOR SALVATION

The panicked actions of people can be perfect examples of the point at which denial becomes like a drowning man grasping for a life raft. At this stage, things are falling apart. Consequences of actions that violated your essential values, long deferred by last-ditch actions and cobbled-together solutions, are finally coming to pass. When you grasp for salvation, you take whatever rope is thrown to you, because no drowning man pushes away aid. Even if that aid comes with many conditions and promises little more than short-term solace for your wounds, you're taking it.

The third-worst thing about this stage in the decline process is that it often brings with it the beginnings of serious consequences for past actions in the pursuit of more. Divorces occur. Families fracture. Lawsuits get filed. Pink slips appear.

The second-worst thing about this stage is that it represents the point at which many people make the choice to go down with the ship rather than learn from their mistakes. Grasping for salvation does not mean you find it; it means you reach for ever-more-frantic means of recapturing what you had while knowing that it's likely gone forever. Most companies cannot come back from this point, because with the complexity of a corporate structure comes the inability to turn the corporate *culture* in a new direction. Inertia is too strong. The course to ruin is often set.

With individuals, it's different—or it can be different. At this stage, some people will experience a wake-up call and reverse course. They will accept responsibility for their poor choices and deal with the consequences. They will gain clarity on their *why* and learn from their mistakes.

The difference between stepping back from the edge and falling right into the abyss often hinges on the support a person has at home and in the community. Individuals who have managed to maintain strong family or church connections can sometimes find people to anchor them and support them as they make choices that can lead to difficult results: debt, unemployment and more.

But the absolute *worst* thing about this stage is that it's not always different. An equal number of people will fail to turn back from the brink of personal catastrophe, which is really what this stage represents. Those who have alienated most of the best people in their lives fare badly. Alone in their pursuit of more, they are alone in their fall from grace. This is the stage at which some thoroughly corrupted individuals, unable to turn away from the distorted view of themselves, will stubbornly follow their previous path straight to Hell.

This is where some people become completely lost. They vanish into greed, envy, bitterness, corruption or desperation. They reach for any and all fixes for their problems, which usually means selling out the last of their principles and surrendering the last shreds of their previous selves. This is where we see men and women bet the pension fund or sell everything that isn't nailed down. The journey is complete. Jedi knight has become Sith Lord.

People in this stage will often take predictable actions, including:

- Bargaining with superiors for leniency
- Trying to connect with individuals who want nothing to do with them but have useful connections
- Burning up assets that they should be preserving
- Taking wild swings at far-fetched schemes that have slim potential to solve the problems they created

Grasping for salvation is the turning point for anyone facing the choice between what and how and *why*. At some moment in this stage, everyone faces a stark choice: turn your back on everything you have been doing that you knew all along was wrong, or go all-in on your greed, self-hatred and panic.

CAPITULATION TO IRRELEVANCE OR DEATH

The doors close. The bankruptcy sale occurs. People pack up their desks and say their goodbyes. This stage is about endings. When a company fails to pull back from the abyss in the Grasping for Salvation stage, it concludes an inexorable slide by either becoming irrelevant or nonexistent. When this happens to a person who has utterly lost touch with his underlying meaning and purpose, it signals the beginning of the end of life as he knows it. It's a sad stage marked in some cases by imprisonment of the mind and spirit (and sometimes, the body) and the loss of everything that ever had any meaning.

At this stage, all hope is essentially lost—at least, all hope of preserving what was built by the previous years of hard work, sacrifice and expense. Because all that work and cost was based on a false premise—I am what I earn and own—and it all comes crumbling down. The previous stage is the final opportunity to pull oneself away from the precipice. This process of decline is like a spacecraft falling into a black hole: as long as it stays outside of the event horizon, it can still escape as long as it applies enough engine thrust. But once it crosses the event horizon, no force in the universe can rescue it from destruction. This stage of Collins' process lies across the event horizon for both companies and individuals. There's no going back.

I'm concerned with the lone man or woman in conflict with himself or herself. For us, capitulation takes one of two forms: Death or Zombie.

- **Death**—I'm not talking about the actual cessation of life, although that does happen from time to time. We've heard the stories about stockbrokers and the like who've taken dives out of 30th-floor windows when their assets hit rock bottom. But most of the time, in this context, death has nothing to do with the well-named "dirt nap." It's the death of everything in the person's former life that made it worth having. Death is the demise of that life in its entirety: the loss of family, dissolution of wealth, termination of position, fracturing of mental and physical health, and loss of station and respect.

  Most people who fall to this stage will see everything they thought was important taken away from them by force or circumstance. They'll hit bottom. This can be the beginning of a rebound, but it's a costly lesson that destroys everything you've built over 30 years and forces you to start over again with no support, no family and no credibility.

- **Zombie**—In this situation, the person in question doesn't realize that everything has fallen apart. He may still have his position and his family may still be intact. But there's no life or growth in any of it. It's undead. His job is stripped of any opportunity for advancement, his family situation is quietly poisonous, and he's so leveraged that the slightest financial setback will bring down the whole house of cards. His life still seems to be proceeding on track, but it's not.

This is actually a more disturbing, sad turn of events than death, because you're irrelevant. Your work doesn't matter. You're not making people around you better, and you're not inspiring anyone. You serve nothing, not even yourself. But because you don't have the dramatic destruction of death to shake you from your stupor, there's nothing to make you realize you have to change things. You just struggle on in a state of delusion, slowly decaying like one of the walking dead.

There aren't any real signs that you're headed into this final stage. By the time you get there, it's too late. Any chance you had to pull yourself back from the brink evaporated long before. The only thing you can do is hang on and try to minimize your losses and learn from your hard experience.

If you see some similarities between my description of these five stages and your own pursuit of success, odds are you're not at the extreme end of the scale where things are falling apart. Most of the people I meet who have lost sight of *why* are somewhere between Hubris and Denial. They are unhappy but don't understand the reason; they feel sick inside but not sick enough to turn their backs on their choices in order to reconnect with their purpose and meaning.

That's good news. It means that you have time to reverse course and ask the hard questions that produce real change. If, on the other hand, you have avoided the trap of chasing what and how and you have oriented your life's pursuits on *why*, then bravo to you. You have found wisdom. Now, let's take a closer look at how we change our behavior so that we can dwell in the heart of meaning and purpose.

Chapter 4

DON'T CHANGE YOUR ACTION, CHANGE YOUR THINKING

"Men are anxious to improve their circumstances, but are unwilling to improve themselves; they therefore remain bound."

—JAMES ALLEN, *AS A MAN THINKETH*

Years ago, my marriage was on the edge of failure. I had spent years in my own Undisciplined Pursuit of More, chasing Wholesaler of the Year honors, money and influence. I didn't get married until I was 36 years old, and after a little more than a year, with a new baby on board, my marriage was failing.

The great Broadway composer Stephen Sondheim once wrote in a lyric, "There are only two worthwhile things to leave behind when you depart this world of ours: children and art." Well, once you strip away all the charades and meaningless stuff, there are only two things in this life that are truly important. One is *honor*. Set aside titles, education, income, family background, even name—all the things that define our identities—and the self comes down to one issue: whether or not you are someone who does what you say you will do. If you are, then you have honor.

The second is *the people who love you*. In his poem *The Death of the Hired Man*, Robert Frost wrote, "Home is the place where, when you have to go there, They have to take you in." The people who love you are the ones who will always take you in. They might be family or friends; it doesn't matter. And that's it. Those are all we have at the end of the day: those who see the good in us and that which *defines* the good in us.

Well, I was busy burning through both of those vital resources at a record-breaking clip. Not only was I watching my family life turn to ashes, but I was failing to uphold my promise to put my wife and newborn son first in my priorities. But today, I remain not only married and happy, but ecstatically content with my family life. How did that happen?

When I speak about this at events, I share with my audiences that part of my salvation was that my wife got me to seek therapy to deal with some longstanding emotional baggage. Then I ask them how they thought my wife got me to seek help. The most frequent answer is that she threatened to leave me. But that's the answer of anger and self-righteousness, and therefore the wrong answer. If my wife had confronted me, told me I was the bad guy, and said I needed to see a therapist or she'd take our son and go, what do you think I would have done?

Exactly. I would have reacted with anger and defensiveness. We'd be divorced now. I would be alone. But my wife was much wiser than that. Instead of threatening me, she did the only thing that could have worked: *she got help herself*. She led by example. When she eventually asked me to seek help, she did not ask me to do something she was not doing. Faced with her courage, I had no choice.

THOUGHT CHANGES INSTANTLY

What my wife did was not change my action, but my thinking. If she'd threatened me, I might have gone to therapy, but it would have been with an arms-crossed, defiant, "you're not going to get me to admit anything" attitude. My action would have changed, but my thinking would have remained exactly the same. Nothing would have been accomplished.

Instead, my wife's action forced me to reassess my own thought process. When I did that, I was able to see how badly I had jumped the tracks of my life. As financial advisor Bill Koontz says, "It's not how much money you have, it's how much heart you have. Because of our culture, if you are not careful, you will develop an inverse relationship between the two." I went to therapy with an open heart and I was able to benefit from it. Everything changed for the better.

When you change your action without changing your thought, the action is unsustainable. Human beings cannot continue a course of action if their course of thinking is opposed to that action. That's why so many millions of people are yo-yo dieters. They change their eating habits for a time but fail to change their underlying thinking about food and exercise. Their lack of self-esteem or their self-pity will often lead them right back into overeating. They treat the symptom, not the disease. As a result, they eventually revert to old habits and gain back all the weight they lost.

Some people are motivated by what and how. Others are not just motivated, but inspired by why. Those who are motivated by what and how tend to take actions that elevate their results. More money, more power, more acclaim—those are results that change nothing about the person behind them. That makes them unsustainable. People motivated and inspired by *why*, on the other hand, tend to choose actions that elevate *themselves*—that fundamentally improve or transform who they are at a basic level. They know that when you improve the person, the results inevitably follow, and those results are more sustainable.

The trouble is, we tend to perceive the path of self-enlightenment and self-improvement as a slow path. We look at kung fu students taking years to master self-denial at Buddhist monasteries and think, *Screw that. I'm not waiting ten years to get that corner office.* So we go after results. You could say that to get the corner office we're willing to cut corners. But the truth is, thoughts can change on a dime. Being exposed to the right situation or behavior can immediately transform your thinking. That's what happened to me when my wife challenged me by getting help for herself. Bang! My thinking shifted. My results changed, though the ultimate results took more time.

NEW YEAR'S RESOLUTIONS

Believe it or not, 87% of New Year's Resolutions are broken by Valentine's Day.[19] According to a 2002 study[20] published in the *Journal of Clinical Psychology*, 23% of them, are broken after one week, which may include those who have changed their goals, rather then dropped their resolution. That's some serious incongruity. That's millions of people who are resolving to change their results, but doing nothing about changing themselves.

Why does that occur? Because we are focusing on what and how, not why. If my doctor tells me that I need to lose 50 pounds in order to bring down my cholesterol and avoid developing Type 2 diabetes, I have two choices. I can look in the mirror and face the reasons *why* I became 50 pounds overweight in the first place, or I can just start Jenny Craig and buy a home treadmill. Which path do you think will more likely yield long-term success?

Obviously, it's the *why* path. But that path entails pain. It's hard to admit that you're addicted to junk food or that you binge because your father always told you that you were fat. It's not about changing the way you think about food, but the way you think about *yourself.*

It might be less effective in the long run to just change behavior, but it's also easier and a heck of a lot less painful. Most of the time, that's what we'll choose. Most people don't even make New Year's resolutions anymore because they know they'll break them, and they don't want the hit to their self-esteem. We don't even bother.

We all want to get greater results. But that breeds the question, "What do we need to do in order to get?" That's the question I hear at Jackson National Life all the time. We've been exceptionally successful at a time when many firms have gone out of business. What do other companies do differently? Here's the answer:

It doesn't matter.

Disciplined action without disciplined thought is a recipe for disaster. It's not what the successful person does that gets the result. It's who the successful person is. It's not the action that "gets" the result. It's the thought process that leads to actions—actions that are in harmony with the person's character and purpose. "What do I do in order to get?" is the wrong question. Here's the right question:

Who must I become in order to change my actions?

In order to change who you are, you must change your thinking. It's that simple and that complex at the same time. That's the fruit and root of my thinking. The self-help industry in the United States—books, CDs, seminars, retreats, you name it—is worth about $12 billion. And most of it is worthless, except to the coaches and authors who are raking in the money. Why? Because it's about 15 steps to this, ten steps to that. It's primarily about changing behavior! If your action is focused on circumstances, and not on yourself, you will not change anything.

FIVE STEPS TO CHANGING YOUR THINKING

You might find it humorous that I beat up the idea of "X steps" in the last paragraph, only to present my own step-based solution here. Well, it's not the idea of a step-oriented process that's the problem. It's the content of that process; it's what it asks you to address. If it asks you to address your behavior without first going after the thought processes behind that behavior, then you're probably wasting your time. You'll lose 25 pounds and then in a year, gain it all back plus a special bonus five.

This process hacks into the brain to attack the processes that blind us to the need to focus on who we are and not what we do. If you follow it to its conclusion, I can't promise that you'll find enlightenment or perfect happiness. I can promise that you'll know more about yourself, why you've made choices in the past, and maybe how you can transform your mind going forward.

These are the five steps in this process:

1. Admit the lies you've been telling yourself.
2. Recalibrate your pleasure center to the intrinsic and long-term.
3. Do what demands the most courage.
4. Become aware of your own thinking.
5. Induce a crisis.

1. Admit the Lies You've Been Telling Yourself

We all tell ourselves lies. Even if your life seems relatively satisfying, with a solid job and a great family, there are undoubtedly areas that are not perfect. Perhaps you are not in the greatest physical condition. Maybe your relationship with your parents or siblings is strained or worse. It's possible you're deep in debt with no apparent way out. There are many ways for dark clouds to block the sun from our lives.

Whatever clouds are darkening your life, they were almost certainly guided there (at least in part) by lies that you have told yourself over the years and come to believe. Everyone does it. We all have a few comforting falsehoods that allow us to deny responsibility for the things about ourselves or our situations that aren't right. A few of the blockbusters:

- I'm overweight because I have a thyroid problem.
- I never finished college because I'm dyslexic.
- My spouse just won't open up and I don't understand why.
- I don't know where all the money goes each month.
- That Facebook conversation with my ex is innocent flirtation.
- My kid won't talk to me because teenagers are just difficult.
- I don't know why my father wouldn't open up to me at the end of his life.

You can probably think of a bunch more on your own. Maybe you've heard friends utter them and rolled your eyes. That's the irony: we can recognize self-delusion in others but we refuse to see it in ourselves. That's also the great problem: we don't even admit that we have a problem. We don't admit that we're engaging in deliberate, long-term self-delusion to protect ourselves.

To protect ourselves from what? From the *pain of regret*. My friend Rob Holdford, whose book, *LIFEonomics*, I mentioned earlier, wrote about this extensively. To summarize, he argued that human consciousness will do anything to avoid the pain of regret—past choices that, by definition, we cannot change.

Let's say you're a guy who's obese and has hypertension and diabetes. In reality, a big reason that you're in such sad shape is because you developed a dysfunctional relationship with food to deal with your pain at being the klutz in a family of athletic brothers. To comfort yourself, you ate. When you got fat, nobody expected you to be a great athlete, so you were off the hook. That thinking persisted into adulthood and so did your weight. But looking truthfully at that reality is painful. It hurts to face the pain of your family situation and accept responsibility for your choices. So you come up with a comforting lie. It's your thyroid. It's your metabolism. Anything to avoid dealing with the agonizing truth and being accountable to it.

It doesn't matter if you're a triathlete. The same dynamic plays out with respect to family, money, marriage, career, you name it. Most of us have comforting self-delusions that we cling to because owning up to the truth—that we're largely responsible for the bad situation because of our poor choices or our cowardice—is just too much to deal with. It's a blow to our self-esteem that we'd rather dodge. So we perpetuate the dysfunction.

Guess what? The first step to changing your thinking is the hardest one: *getting past the lies.* That means looking at whatever problem defines your life and asking, "What did I do to cause this?" Because, odds are, you brought most of the difficulty on yourself. Now, it's possible that your marriage is failing because your spouse cheated on you and you're blameless, but most of the time that's just not true. Most of the time, we're complicit in our own downfall.

Until you can look in the mirror, see the lies for what they are, and accept responsibility for the role that your thinking—your choices—have played in creating the situation, there's no hope. You'll change actions, but you won't change your thoughts. It's liberating when you finally face up to the past. Suddenly, you're able to admit your sins to yourself (and maybe even to others), and you see that doing so doesn't destroy you!

Yes, it hurts to do this. That's why we avoid it in the first place! But we do that because of the misguided notion that avoiding accountability will save our self-esteem. It's not true. The deeper self always knows that we're being cowardly. That self-delusion actually eats away at self-esteem. But when you find the courage to shed the lies and deal with the uncomfortable truth, you may hurt, but you will also feel pride. You will know you've done the hard thing, the brave thing. That's a gift in itself. You will know you've taken the first step toward changing your thinking permanently. That's freedom.

2. Recalibrate Your Pleasure Instinct To The Intrinsic And Long-Term

There's a controversial quote often attributed to model Kate Moss that goes like this: "Nothing tastes as good as thin feels." That's a perfect encapsulation of this step. When you read interviews with people who have managed to lose a lot of weight and get truly fit (I keep coming back to weight and fitness because it's near-universal), a common theme emerges: they learned to take pleasure in the workouts, in eating right, in being virtuous.

That's what I'm talking about here. Once you've faced the lies you've been telling yourself, the next step in changing your thinking is recalibrating your pleasure center. It's had a lot do to with getting you so far away from the life you want. For example, let's say you're deep in debt. You owe tens of thousands on credit cards and you're near bankruptcy. Yet you make plenty of money, so what's the problem?

When you stop lying to yourself, you can see how you're culpable: you buy lots of expensive toys. To get even more basic, the act of buying a 64-inch plasma TV with surround sound gives you more pleasure than the act of paying down your credit card balance, even though you know that paying down debt is what you should be doing. In this way, we make foolish choices because we're addicted to the dopamine hit, that spark in the brain's pleasure center.

If you're going to change your thinking, you have to retrain your brain to take pleasure in things that are intrinsic and long-term, rather than things that are extrinsic and short-term.

- *Intrinsic, long-term things* affect your character, your sense of purpose and your passion, and tend to deliver rewards that are not immediate but come over time and are sustainable. Examples: training to run a marathon, paying off your debts with a multi-year plan, going to marriage counseling.

- *Extrinsic, short-term things* affect the material trappings of your life or your senses, and tend to deliver rewards that are instantaneous but brief. Examples: eating a whole box of Oreos, buying a boat with your home equity line, having an affair.

To have a prayer of changing your circumstances you must train yourself to take greater pleasure in the intrinsic and long-term than in the extrinsic and short-term. That means getting a bigger buzz from working out and doing something great for your heart than from eating a pizza. It means getting greater satisfaction from putting money into your IRA than in blowing it on a new computer. It's all right to have those things once in a while, but they can't be your major source of joy.

Basically, following this step means finding satisfaction in virtue and wisdom. It's not easy, but it's possible. People recalibrate their pleasure instinct all the time. It's a matter of taking the virtuous action, then reflecting on how great it feels while you resist taking the foolish, shortsighted action. Send off a deposit to your 401(k) and think about how great it makes you feel to do that instead of wasting your money on something else. Do that in multiple areas of your life and over time you'll begin enjoying the intrinsic stuff more than the extrinsic. That's a huge step in changing your thinking!

3. Do What Demands the Most Courage

I've written about the amygdala a great deal and I speak about it often. It's the center in the brain that's responsible for our fear and rage. But the fear that the amygdala lets loose—the panicked, adrenaline-surge fear—is not the kind of fear I'm talking about here. I'm talking about fear that's more considered. This is fear that overturns your previous way of doing things and leaves no road back.

For all of us, persistent self-delusion disguises something that we dread. When we dread something, we avoid it at all costs because confronting it reveals truths that we would rather not know about. For example, part of the reason that I drove myself to such excesses of work and ambition (to the point where I nearly destroyed my marriage) was to prove that I was not like my father, who abandoned me. But over the years, I never did what took the greatest courage, which was to learn about my father and find out why he did what he did.

Why did I avoid that? Because if I had found out that my father wasn't a loser, but just a human being who had made a poor decision in a moment of weakness, that would have taken away the justification for all the hours I was working and all the money I was making to the detriment of my family life. It would have forced me to confront the real reason behind my behavior: that I was basing my worth on my net worth. I didn't want to face that reality, so I avoided learning anything about my father.

But eventually, after I went to therapy to save my marriage, I reconnected with my father. I learned that he wasn't a loser, just a flawed man like the rest of us. Now, he and I are close. If I had gained that knowledge when I was still a success-at-all-costs guy, it might have been too much to bear. I would have had to accept full responsibility for my choice to emotionally abandon my own family to chase money and position.

After you have faced up to your self-delusions and started training yourself to take more pleasure in doing the right thing, it's time to do the one thing that demands the most courage. Notice that I didn't write, "Do the thing you're most afraid of." The two are different. Doing what you fear the most is often simply a matter of closing your eyes and getting through it, as in skydiving. You don't necessarily gain any insight.

But doing what demands courage is a conscious act of facing and accepting not only what scares you, but *why* it scares you. An act of courage is a positive step that opens your eyes. It might be going for a physical after years of being overweight and out of shape. It might be calling the brother you haven't talked to in 20 years and patching things up. It could be cutting up your credit cards.

Your act that takes the most courage is something that you consider carefully and then do despite your fear, and it changes you. Suddenly, you wonder what you were so afraid of. The fact is, the fears in our own minds are *always* far greater than the reality when things are said and done. You might fear that at your physical your doctor will tell you that you have diabetes. But in all likelihood, she won't. Reality shrinks the fear we carry within us. We feel slightly foolish, and then we realize we are no longer afraid. That's one more step in the right direction.

4. Become Aware of Your Own Thinking

By the third step, you've done a good job of purging your system, or if you prefer, reformatting your inner hard drive. You've confronted your lies, started taking pleasure in the things that make you better as a person, and you have acted with courage. Great! But what's to stop you from acting like a yo-yo dieter and repeating your whole dysfunctional pattern all over again?

It's called *metacognition*. Basically, that's a fancy term for being able to watch yourself think in real time. A person with metacognition has a sort of dual consciousness: the mind that works its way through daily life by making choice after choice, and a sort of higher mind that stands back and says, "Hmm, why did I do that? Was I acting out of fear, or did I really believe what I said? What did I expect the result to be?"

Metacognition is an extremely sophisticated state of awareness that's critical for self-improvement. It doesn't mean that you second-guess everything that you do or that you should over-think every choice, but that you are always aware of your motivations for thinking, speaking and acting as you do. You're always checking yourself for self-delusion. You're always monitoring whether or not your thoughts and behaviors are in line with your character and morals.

Can you see why such a high level of self-awareness would be helpful in not sliding back into self-delusional, short-term behavior? Once you escape from that prison and are able to find the self-love and confidence to be accountable and deal with your fears, metacognition helps you recognize any old, unhealthy thinking and quash it.

Pangs of guilt? Nope, you're on top of them and know they're illusory. Desires to chase short-term pleasure at the expense of what you know you should do? You can spot that impulse a mile away. Metacognition means you're always improving. It's a fantastic tool.

To begin developing more of it, simply start analyzing the decisions you make or actions you take. Wait until you have some quiet time to really think, and then put your motivations and attitudes under a microscope. Why did you do what you did? Were you serving love or fear? Were you being true to yourself or to what others expected of you? The more you practice this, the more instinctive it will become, until you find that you're able to maintain that high-level split consciousness all the time.

5. Induce a Crisis

I've talked about "hacking the epiphany" and setting off a deliberate existential crisis in your life, and this is the time to do both. You have all this new awareness and new tools, but odds are you're still in much the same boat in your life. That's because your situation doesn't depend solely on you. It also depends on your spouse and kids, on your boss and co-workers, on your friends, on the bank that holds your mortgage or the church you attend each Sunday.

If you genuinely want to change things, you need to take that final step and force life's hand. You need to manufacture a crisis that will give your new courage, awareness and discipline the room to work and create a new direction. A crisis forces you to confront things you haven't yet confronted, take a new direction in your life or career, or make massive changes to your lifestyle.

Since most people don't willingly step out of their comfort zone, this is where I suggest shaking things up on purpose. Some examples of an induced crisis:

- Quitting your job
- Going to therapy
- Confessing to an affair
- Relocating
- Investigating a new religion
- Ending a relationship
- Going back to school

A self-induced crisis should leave you no way back, force you to exorcise the last demons you've been avoiding, and most important, open your eyes to new passions, desires or capabilities you didn't know you had in you. It's the "leap before you look" method of self-improvement, and if you have gone through the first four steps of this process, you're ready to handle it. In fact, you'll relish it because you know that no matter what happens, you will come through it and be a wiser person with a completely different mode of thinking.

That's magic.

Chapter 5

The Moving Walkway

Apart from the known and the unknown, what else is there?

—HAROLD PINTER, PLAYWRIGHT

No matter how much success you've had in your life, there is another level. We each need to look at transforming not only our circumstances but also ourselves. When the individual becomes different, his circumstances, over time, automatically change.

Seems simple, but it's not. There's a powerful reason why such change is rare, and I'm going to talk about it in this chapter. Imagine a moving walkway at the airport. If you're seeking efficiency, you get on that walkway. If you're in a hurry, you run on it. It gives you a little more speed. But on a typical airport moving walkway, you can see the destination. You can see gate C3, right?

But imagine that there's a moving walkway that led into complete darkness. You can't see a thing about where you're headed. Maybe it's even taking you into a cave, with no signs to tell you what lies ahead. Would you get on that moving sidewalk with the same kind of enthusiasm?

You're already on it. Throughout history, the greatest fear of all human beings is the fear of death. It's the core fear that underlies all the other fears, such as the fear of flying or the fear of snakes. We among all the animals have the unique blessing and curse of consciousness and self-awareness. With them, we can do things that are nearly godlike: project ourselves forward in time to look at our possible future, speculate on possible disasters and take steps to avoid them, cast ourselves backward into time and learn from past mistakes. With our amazing minds, we can transcend time and space.

Yet this same faculty also means that we are (as far as we know) the only creatures on this planet who are aware of the fact that we are finite. Horses, dogs, birds—they all live in the present moment, with no fear of death or awareness of it. But humans can look into our futures, and if we do so far enough, what do we see? The end. We don't know when it will come or how it will come, and we don't really know what will happen afterward, but we know that at some point, we will cease to be. That's a great incongruity that defines us and has shaped our art and our theology. Death is the great mystery.

Sure, you hear that more people are afraid of public speaking than of death. Folks, fear of public speaking is the fear of death. We are herd animals; anyone who becomes separated from the herd is at risk of being killed. Well, what is public speaking but the deliberate act of one person separating herself from the herd? The audience has safety in numbers; the speaker is on the stage, exposed. She could be picked off at any time by a leopard. Of course, that's not likely to happen in a modern auditorium, but the amygdala, the primitive part of the brain, doesn't know that! Thus, it reacts with fear.

THE UNKNOWN FUTURE

Where is death for all of us? In the unknown future. So it makes sense that we all have a primordial fear of that unknown future. Most human beings don't operate well on unknowns. We crave input, data, or at least plausible speculation. It's no wonder that over the centuries, people have paid a lot of attention to—and in some cases, a lot of money to—people who claimed to have accurate information about what was going to happen in the future.

We've called them palm readers, shamans, oracles, psychics. Today, we have more sophisticated terms for them: economists, analysts, CNN. The names have changed, but the principle is the same. We want to know what is going to happen because even illusory intelligence about our futures helps quell that death anxiety that all of us face.

The heart of religious practice for most people is about dealing with the fear of the unknown future. Mankind really has two great existential fears:

1. Fear of death
2. Fear of chaos

The fear of death is obvious. We fear death because we don't know for certain what's going to happen after it. Even people with deep religious beliefs and a belief in an afterlife fear death because *what if they're wrong?* Our beliefs reside in the prefrontal cortex of the brain, the seat of our humanity. But as we've seen, the primitive amygdala overrides that sophisticated part of the brain during times of primordial fear. When faced with a survival situation, even people of deep religious faith will act instinctively to preserve their lives. The obvious isn't so obvious in the heat of the moment. That doesn't mean they lack faith in God or don't believe in Heaven. It means they are human.

Some people fear that death is annihilation, the self going out like a candle. Others fear Judgment or Hell. Others fear not so much death but the act of dying. They worry that they will be in pain, lose their dignity, or lose their identity. Religion helps believers deal with those fears by promising salvation after suffering, an eternity of peace and bliss.

But I suggest that an equally deep fear is the fear of chaos—that is, that things happen without a reason. If you look at this world, not only can you conclude that we have no idea what's going to happen in the future, but that there's no rhyme or reason to any of it. Children die in earthquakes. Innocent people go to the gas chamber. Health nuts drop dead from heart attacks at age 50 while smokers live to 103. If we can't know what's going to happen, at least it's comforting to think that there is some grand plan behind it all—God's will, if you like. Without some sense of order to lend structure to the random events of the day—and with the fear of death behind everything—many of us would hide in our beds and never come out.

Look at the evening news. Watch how much predictive behavior is involved. What they are essentially saying is, "This bad stuff happened, so this other bad stuff will continue to happen." It's the selling of fear. Look at the promotional spots for your local news. They never say, "Everything is OK, go to bed." No, they feature a grim-faced anchor saying, "Your blender could kill you. News at eleven." They use fear to get you to stay up and stay involved.

A huge percentage of communication through the mainstream media today is about the marketing of fear. The media makes its money on advertising. During sports events, what are the ads for? Beer, sports, and so on. That's what the audience wants. But on the nightly news, they're for prescription drugs that treat erectile dysfunction, sleeplessness, depression and heart disease. Just by mentioning the odds of someone having heart disease or cancer, these ads create fear and uncertainty. The companies know that's a way to sell products. They know exactly what they are doing!

As a result, and empowered by the Internet, we're becoming a nation of hypochondriacs! And what is hypochondria but the desire to identify a medical condition (even though it's imaginary) in order to keep from dying from it in the unknown future?

Fear of the unknown will stop your self-transformation dead in the water. When I was 42, I was contemplating a speaking career, even though I was already very successful as a financial wholesaler. I got shingles. Now, shingles is normally a disease that hits people over age 65. It's a disease that hits because the immune system is compromised, allowing a virus that's been dormant in the body for decades (if you don't know, it's the same virus that causes chicken pox when you're a kid) to flare up and cause this intense, painful rash.

I developed shingles because I was stressed out, afraid of the unknown. When the body's hit by stress, which is essentially fear, the amygdala sends out signals that shut down the immune system. My thinking, my fear of the unknown future, made me sick! We are all scared to death.

SELF-EFFICACY, NOT SELF-ESTEEM

As we transition into focusing on the potential for self-transformation, this fact—the fear of the unknown—becomes critical. The truth is that most of us can find a comfortable place within the life we're currently leading, even if it's at its root unsatisfying or actively destroying us from within. Why? Because it's known. That's why change is so traumatic for most people—it represents the unknown.

Look at the list of the most traumatic events in people's lives. The ones that usually top the list—the death of a spouse and the death of a child—are understandable. But usually right below those are things like starting a new job and relocating. Why? What's so traumatic about going to work for a new company or moving to a new city? Aren't those exciting opportunities for growth and discovery?

In theory, yes, but in practice, they are huge unknowns! We don't know how we'll fare at a new job…what if we can't cut it? What if we hate our new city? What if the moving truck never shows up? What if the kids' new school is in a gang-ridden area? We can tie ourselves in knots with worries invented to encompass the fear Holy of Holies: *I don't know what's going to happen.*

But just what is this fear all about? Some might say that harboring such relentless fear reflects a profound lack of self-esteem. I disagree. My good friend and coach, psychologist Dr. Roger Hall, also has little regard for the concept of self-esteem. Instead, he talks about the concept called *self-efficacy.*[21] This is a brilliant idea that will change how you perceive yourself and why you hold on to fear about the future.

Self-efficacy is the belief that because you have survived the ups and downs that life has thrown at you in the past, you have the capacity to do so in the future. It's a deep confidence in one's own competence. People with a strong sense of self-efficacy rarely (if ever) even question their ability to handle what life brings their way. *Of course I can handle this.*

While self-esteem can be grounded in meaningless self-talk—the good old "Because I'm good enough, I'm smart enough, and, doggonit, people like me!" Saturday Night Live line—self-efficacy is grounded in good old facts. You had the capability and courage to overcome the odds once, so you can do it again. That's the kind of empowering self-talk that you find in CEOs, professional athletes, and others who have defied the odds to rise to the top of their professions. It's the mentality of being unstoppable.

Can you see how having a self-efficacious mentality would be an advantage in overcoming the fear of the unknown? The problem with the "cult of self-esteem," as author Lori Gottlieb[22] has called it, is that self-esteem is based on factors that are largely external. The way I see it, self-esteem is built on how much other people value you and what you do! It's based on the praise that other people heap upon you and, to a great degree, on your material rewards for all those things you do. *I have this huge house and hot and cold running SUVs, so I must be a worthwhile person!*

But remember, measuring your worth by your net worth is a sure path to feeling worth-less. You have no control over the things people say or think about you. As we have witnessed over the past few years, circumstances can strip us of our homes, cars and other possessions very quickly. Actions that draw praise from others can in the long run turn out to be destructive, such as unethical or illegal acts that enrich a company but in the end destroy it. Self-esteem is a castle built on damp, unstable soil. It's prone to instability and is easily overthrown.

Self-efficacy is nothing like self-esteem, because it's based only on your own cell-deep belief that you have what it takes to be victorious in any circumstance. That doesn't always mean coming out on top in the money or fame race; sometimes, it means having the courage to stick to your principles and do what's right even under pressure to do otherwise. Because it's built on internal evidence and sense of self, it's unassailable. If you have a strong sense of self-efficacy, there is little anyone can do to change that. If your net worth drops or certain people hold a negative opinion of you, it doesn't matter. You know that you have what it takes to do well and to do good.

YOU ARE THE WHY

If you're in fear, you won't walk through the door of self-transformation and get to even one or two of those steps I describe in Chapter Four. Transformation and change are uncertain and therefore terrifying; when you leave your secure job in order to start your own business, you walk out on a high wire with no net. If you fall, your family loses its home and your kids don't go to college. So taking the steps that lead to a change in your character demands that you overcome fear.

Getting past empty self-esteem to believe in your own self-efficacy is the way to make that happen. If you have a strong sense of your own capacity to handle a crisis and make the right calls, then you will have far less fear about the future. When I speak to financial advisors, I tell them that their clients are not buying their *competence*, but their *confidence*. It's the faith in the advisor's efficacy that keeps the clients on the path and making smart financial decisions. As soon as they lose faith, they're gone. Their fear takes over. As Charles Kettering said, "No one would have crossed the ocean if he could have gotten off the ship in the storm."

You have to have that kind of absolute faith in yourself if you're going to make the kinds of radical shifts in your thinking that will lead to true success. This is why my focus on *why* is so critical. You cannot establish that beachhead of enormously strong self-efficacy at your core if you try to base it on what you're doing and how you're doing it. Why? Because there's always going to be someone who's more talented or skilled than you are. There will always be goals you don't reach or work you do that doesn't meet somebody's standards. Focusing what and how puts your sense of capability in the hands of other people, and *they don't care about you*. They will discard your best efforts not out of malice but out of dismissal, and you'll be devastated by that.

Building your self-efficacy on *why* changes things. It gives you back your power. Doing this means developing a sense of your own capacity to endure, achieve and stay on your ethical true north—always by focusing on the reasons you do what you do, your own moral center, and the nature of your character. In a sense, we must be the *why* of what we do, because in the short term the *how* and *what* can give us terrible results. If you want to lead a company and you stick to your ethical guns even under pressure to discard them, other people may leap past you…temporarily. But in the long run, that why-first approach will bring you to your goal and give you the strength of character to stay in that corner office.

Disabled triathlete Jason Lester is a terrific example of building self-efficacy by building on why, not what and how. In his book, *Running on Faith*,[23] he relates how, after losing the use of his right arm at age twelve, he fell in love with triathlons after seeing the Ironman World Championships in Hawaii. Convinced that God had called him to inspire others by becoming a successful endurance athlete despite his handicap, Jason trained and persevered and eventually became the first person with a disability to finish the punishing Ultraman race, a double-length Ironman that forces competitors to swim 6.2 miles.

Imagine swimming six miles with one arm! I can't even imagine swimming that far with two arms! Yet if Jason had focused on what and how, he probably would have failed. After all, he was trying to swim that far with only half the propulsion of able-bodied competitors, and bike more than 200 miles to boot. The obstacles were overwhelming, yet he kept his focus on *why* he was subjecting himself to the agony of such a race: he was serving God's purpose and trying to inspire millions of others with disabilities. In the end, he not only completed the race but also went on to become one of the leading ultra-endurance athletes in the country.

That's self-efficacy. That's the belief that "I have what it takes." That's what your transformation of self will rest on.

FOCUS ON HOPE

There's this odd idea that worrying is the mature thing to do. People who look for the positive side are hit with pejoratives like "Pollyanna" or "you have your head in the clouds." I'm going to talk more about this later in the book, but for our discussion of fear, it's appropriate to touch on it.

Worry is, at its core, the belief that you don't have what it takes to deal with whatever comes along in the uncertain future. It's an indictment of your self-efficacy. If you have the strength, skill and courage to overcome obstacles, why worry? So if you're fearful, you must not have those qualities, right? It's a self-filling pit of quicksand that paralyzes us.

Yet we persist in focusing on fear and our likely inability to make the best of whatever circumstances come our way in the future. We do this, I believe, because of a misguided belief that worrying *about* the future somehow equals preparation *for* the future. But that's simply untrue. If we worry about the unknown, unknowable future, we hamstring our ability to muster the love, hope and courage to deal with it, whatever it may be. As author and bishop E. Bernard Jordan writes, "Fear is a useless emotion." Yet we feel that fear is the mature, grownup way to deal with the future. If we insist on being hopeful about the future because we have the tools to make it what we want it to be, then we're being childish, according to popular thought.

Well, what do I always say? The majority is always wrong…eventually. The worriers might feel like they are being wise and realistic and prepared, but in fact, they are crippling their self-efficacy. To be able to take the steps toward truly changing your thinking and ultimately your circumstances, you must take a different path:

Move your attention from fear of the future to hope for it.

I like to think of the negative, self-defeating, fear-based view of the unknown as a hungry animal. If you continue to shovel fear and worry at that animal, it devours it and demands more…and it grows. It's always starving and will eat all the fear you can deliver. But if you orient your mind on hope—on the self-efficacy that says, "I can come out on top in any situation"—then you deny the animal your attention and your fear. You starve the beast. Divert your attention from fear long enough and the beast dies.

The thing is, that beast can only live as long as you feed it. But as long as you do, it will keep eating. When you deny it, it will howl. It will roar. That's your fear coming for you, trying to talk you into putting it front and center in your view of the future. But the more you resist, the weaker the fear becomes. Eventually, you can't hear it at all.

If you want to develop the self-efficacy that overcomes fear and empowers you to do just about anything, orient on hope. Forget about worry. You can do two things with what happens: prepare for it and respond to it. That's it. If you're prepared and know how to respond in a positive way, what's to fear?

Chapter 6

Your IRA and Your IAR

*It had long since come to my attention that people of
accomplishment rarely sat back and let things happen
to them. They went out and happened to things.*

—LEONARDO DA VINCI

You're probably thinking, "Steve, all this talk about self-transformation and changing my thinking is great, but how do I do it? How do I do the heavy lifting of switching up how my mind works after umpteen years of being the way I am?" I understand. It's not an easy thing to do. That's why earlier I spoke about the self-induced crisis. A crisis gives you no choice but to change how you think and act. It shocks you into doing things differently. But not only is it difficult to bring on a crisis, who wants to live that way? It should not be necessary to invite chaos and pain into your life for the purpose of living better. That's like breaking your own legs in the hope that when they heal, you'll be taller.

You're in luck. I have some specific tools I want to share in the second half of this book. To look at the first, let's consider something. Each of us is born with an IRA. Now, I'm not talking about the Individual Retirement Account (though it would be pretty cool to come out of the womb with $20,000 already earning interest). I'm talking about three states of mind:

Intention

Retention

Attention

You can imagine them in a circle like this one:

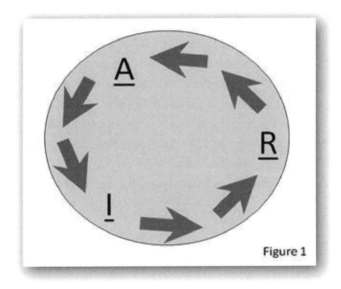

Figure 1

We all come from the factory wired this way. The brain's intention is the retention of what it has already learned. That's our default setting. Some people define it as "continuity of consciousness." When you go to bed at night, you retain what you learned during the previous days and years of your life. When I get up in the morning, I don't have to relearn how to open and drink a bottle of water, brush my teeth or drive my car. I can do those things *unconsciously*, and that's a key paradox here. Our minds are compelled to hang on to the things they have already learned…so that we can live unconsciously! Now who believes that unconscious living is ever better than conscious living? William Wordsworth said, "But habit rules the unreflecting herd," while Socrates said,

"The unexamined life is not worth living." Now, who's going to argue with Wordsworth and Socrates?

Unfortunately, we're wired to establish habits and not to reflect upon them. From an evolutionary perspective, this was a matter of survival. We adopted those habits that preserved our lives. Now, one of the ways the brain retains the information that it wants to retain is by focusing its attention on that which strengthens retention. People who drive more often become better drivers than people who don't drive as much, because they are getting more feedback each time they drive. They narrowly miss an accident, and they store and retain that information over the long term.

As you study and learn over time, you retain more. You become an expert in certain areas. That has really propelled your life in a lot of ways. It may have enabled you to become proficient enough in a field to become a professional at it and earn a living doing it. If you think about premier professional fields like law or medicine, they are largely about the retention of vast amounts of information created by others over time—organic chemistry and biological facts on one hand, case law and legal precedent on the other. So this IRA structure, in which the mind's awareness flows around the circle in a counter-clockwise direction, is pretty useful.

THE INDIVIDUAL REGRET ACCOUNT

But it's also limiting you and what you can achieve. You are also retaining things that you want to forget. When you allow your mind to operate unconsciously in this way, you are filling up your Individual Regret Account. In addition, you are also retaining beliefs that are not true, mostly about what you can accomplish. In this way, we set our own limits.

Thomas Edison said, "If we did all the things we are capable of, we would literally astound ourselves." But we don't think like that, because that worry impulse tells us that believing that we are unstoppable is naïve and childish. So we coast. We allow our minds to lock on to retention of what we already know and, in doing so, we ignore the acquisition of the new, fresh and challenging. But behind that, we have a massive capability that we have not yet tapped. We also have an Individual Resistance Account. We resist change, because change is the death of something!

When we change something such as our house, car or job, that change reminds us of the impermanence of things, and that reminds us of our own impermanence—that one day we won't be here. The brain doesn't want to go in the direction of death, so it takes the path of least resistance, which is that counter-clockwise direction in which we give our attention to what we already know.

Why do you think we talk about "paying" attention? Because attention is currency. What you focus your attention on, you own. When your mind centers your attention on what you have already learned, that's what you get. It's safe and predictable, and it will get you *nowhere but where you already are today*. If you're paying for it, you get it. Attention is a limited resource; do you really want to use it to buy the life you have today, the one that you so desperately want to change and improve?

The greatest get-rich scheme is to change the way you think. What good is it to have a billion dollars but feel poor? The rich man has enough; he feels rich. What he has fills him up entirely. Heck, if wealth alone was enough to fill our spirits and make us feel rich, those people on *The Real Housewives of Beverly Hills* wouldn't all be so miserable! When we pay attention to the things that we want to retain—money, skills, power—that's all we get, and it's never enough. The attention of a billionaire has exactly the same purchasing power—no more, no less—than that of a person living in a homeless shelter. Whatever your attention goes to, you own. And if your attention is on lies, emptiness or pain, that's what you'll bring into your life, whether you're financially rich or poor.

"DADDY HAS TO LEAVE"

I've alluded to my abandonment by my father a couple of times, but now it's time to get into the whole story. I was eleven years old, and it was 1974. Up to that time I had lived in Northern Alabama, and I had one sibling, a sister, two years younger. That year, we went on a family vacation down to Florida. I didn't know—couldn't have known—that I would not be coming back from that vacation. It took my best friend 28 years to find me.

On this vacation, in one night, my life changed forever. It was the pivotal moment in my life, and it's why I wrote this book. It fed me a lie that I lived by for 33 years, and if I hadn't learned the truth, I don't know if I'd be alive. I certainly wouldn't have anything to share with you. That night, my father came to me. The lights were out; I was already asleep. He had to wake me. I was disoriented, but I'll never forget being nose-to-nose with him, and what he said to me. He said, "Son, I'm sorry, but Daddy has to leave."

And he was gone. Something more important than his family called to him and I was estranged from him for the next 33 years. I didn't get married until I was 36 years old, and I think that's why. I was paying all my attention to a lie. A girlfriend once said to me, "You don't feel feelings, you *do* feelings." My favorite was the ex-girlfriend who sent me a Christmas card that said, "I hope you have an efficient Christmas." I was so clueless that I thought it was a compliment! I believed that my value was in what I did! Greater efficiency was what I was all about. I had no heart for anyone.

It took me a long time to understand what those comments meant. I was always holding people at arm's length, because, at eleven years old, I'd had my heart ripped out. Remember, this was not a divorce where I was still seeing my dad every other weekend. He was *gone*.

There was a huge dad-sized hole in my heart where he had been, and as I got older, I filled it with work, money and defensiveness. But most of all, I filled it with a lie. The brain hates uncertainty, so it jumps to conclusions. The conclusion—the lie—that my brain gave me was *Your father is a loser.* I had evidence of this: He gave up his wife and his children. The thing is, at 11 years old you're not an adult. You *are* your mother. You *are* your father. Well, if I am my mother, and I am my father, and my father is a loser, then part of me must be a loser!

I spent three decades trying to prove to myself that I wasn't a loser like my father. That's an impossible cup to fill, yet all my attention went into trying to fill it.

Most high achievers are not running to something; they are running *from* something. My early achievements were nothing laudable; when you're running from a lion, you'll outrun everybody. When you make a judgment call, you are blinded by that judgment. Confirmation bias gets in your way. It's a bias that makes you focus on that which confirms your belief. If you believe deep down in your core that a part of you is a loser, or that your value lies only in what you do and what you earn, then your attention will go to those things that confirm that belief. That's what you'll retain. Confirmation bias perpetuates the lies we believe are true. That is what is getting in the way of your next calling.

YOUR IAR

Over your next hurdle, someone is waiting for you to pass them the baton. You have a responsibility and a calling to go to war against anything that might make you less than you are capable of being to embrace the art and not just the science of what you do. You cannot allow anyone to divert your attention by telling you what you are not capable of. *You* decide that!

If you want to buy with your attention that which moves you toward your true calling and to living for your *why*, then you need to open an IAR. The words are the same—intention, attention, retention—but the direction changes. Now you move in the direction of life, not resisting, but embracing. Not filled with lies, fear and hesitation, but with truth, faith and optimism. Now the circle starts at intention and rotates clockwise, like this:

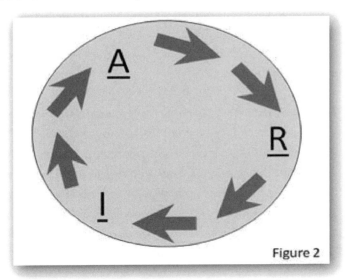

Figure 2

Jim Rohn says, "You cannot change your destination overnight, but you can change your direction overnight." First of all, you wake up with an intention.

With an act of will, you choose to rejoice. You choose to be grateful. You choose where your attention will land at each moment. Tolstoy said that the only place in which you have any power is in the *now*.[24] You can't change the past, and while you can influence the future, your influence over it is centered in how you embrace the now. You do that by living consciously, not unconsciously—by being fully present in the moment and determining where your attention falls.

You intuitively know this. You know that you must address the root, not the tree. Garbage in, garbage out, or great stuff in, great stuff out. IAR stands for:

Individual Achievement Reservoir

By using your intention to focus your attention on that which you choose to retain, you find resources that fill that reservoir. I'm talking about books, magazines, coaches, speakers, mentors—all the factors that help you change your thinking and change your circumstances. You can choose to fill the reservoir with everything that can go wrong or with everything that can go right. Once you let go of the unconscious lies and regrets that send your life in a direction that doesn't match up with your calling, you will begin filling that reservoir with things that do serve that calling.

In his brilliant book, *Thinking, Fast and Slow*, Daniel Kahneman writes about that moment of recognition:[25]

> *The psychology of accurate intuition involves no magic. Perhaps the best short statement of it is by the great Herbert Simon, who studied chess masters and showed that after thousands of hours of practice they come to see the pieces on the board differently from the rest of us. You can feel Simon's impatience with the mythologizing of expert intuition when he writes: "The situation has provided a cue; this cue has given the expert access to information stored in memory, and the information provides the answer. Intuition is nothing more and nothing less than recognition."*

]IAR awareness gives everyone the ability to reach for a higher and improved response to every situation—to be Intentional about where you place your Attention and to place it on what you want to Retain. Intuition can be recalibrated. The jerk in "knee jerk" can be repaired.

Gandhi said, "Be the change that you wish to see in the world." That is about changing your essence, yourself at the core, and letting that fundamental shift change the circumstances around you. Never doubt that this is possible. The entire principle of nonviolent resistance is based on it. How can people who sit peacefully in front of a building or who refuse to give up their seats on a bus be victorious over people with guns and lawyers and prisons? Because the example of *why* moves the minds of others, and changed minds lead to changed circumstances. Only when you become different can you live differently, and only when you think differently can you be different. Steve Jobs had it right.

TOO MUCH SUGAR

I love this story because it's a beautiful example of the awareness of this truth. Here is the foundation of the story. This woman and her child waited in a long line for many hours to see Gandhi. Finally, they got up to the great Mahatma and the woman told him, My son is eating a lot of sugar and has a very poor diet. He won't listen to me about changing his diet, but he will listen to you. Would you please tell him?

The great man thought about this for a moment and then replied, Come back in three days. Well, when Gandhi tells you to come back in three days, you come back in three days. So she left, and three days later, she waited in a long line again, under the hot Indian sun, to see the great man. Finally, she and her son approached, and she said, Mahatma, I don't know if you remember me, but... Gandhi nodded and said, I remember.

Gandhi called the boy to him, placed his hands on the boy's shoulders, and said, Son, stop eating sugar. It's not good for your health. The mother came up to him and said, I appreciate you saying that, but why did you not say that three days ago?

Gandhi looked at her and replied, Because three days ago I was eating sugar. That's integrity. It would have been hypocritical to tell that boy to give up sugar when he himself was eating it![26] Be the change you wish to see in the world.

What changed for me? I finally got help when my wife led the way by changing her own thinking. As a result of that professional assistance, I was finally able to see how I had been letting the lie about my father poison my own life. In trying to prove that I was not a loser, I was focusing my attention on all the wrong things. I was a walking example of excelling at *how* and *what* while failing miserably at *why*. Once I let go of that lie and stopped paying attention to that which confirmed it, I was free.

Today, I have a good relationship with my father. Four years ago, we began to reconcile, and now we communicate regularly. I've come to understand why he did what he did and that he wasn't ever a loser. He was a man navigating the rocks and shoals of his own toxic self-talk and the imperative that told him that self-absorption and the pursuit of more were more important than the love and respect of his wife and children. I remind myself that in striving so hard NOT to make the same choice that he did, I almost made the same terrible mistake he made. So as an adult man, I've been humbled by knowing my dad all over again. I'm grateful for that. But it wouldn't have happened if I hadn't been able to let go of the lies I was feeding myself.

I had to become the change I wanted to see before that change could come about outwardly. That's the power of the IAR. It's conscious, self-aware living that uses the buying power of your attention to buy the things that make you wiser, more empathetic, more loving, more humble and more just.

When we're children, we ask the question "why" all the time. We drive adults crazy asking why the sky is blue and why birds fly. It's part of our nature. But as adults, we rarely ever ask why. We just accept the way things are instead of questioning why they are the way they are. And if we do ask that question, we come up with some empty answer that blames the government, our obligations or the way we were raised. That's wrong. You are the answer; you are sufficient to any question. Everything in your life is a reflection of your thinking. There's no outward cause that has as much power over your circumstances as your mind does.

Ask why. Ask it about everything. Take nothing for granted. When you start doing this, you begin to rotate the IRA wheel in the other direction. You start closing your IRA and opening your IAR, where your deposits are much more likely to deliver the returns you desire.

Start asking why and your intention will begin to direct your attention toward the answers. That will lead you to the next obvious question of "Why not?" As in, "Why not do what I've always dreamed of doing?" or "Why not recapture the enthusiasm for my work that I had when I was 25?" It's not far from those thoughts to seeking out the ideas and resources that can help you make them a reality. That's when you start to fill that reservoir. That's when things start to change and you realize that you're only a prisoner of your thinking until you change your thinking.

What's the story you tell yourself about yourself? Why do you tell it? Is it true? What dark corners do you not allow your mind to go, and why? What do you fear will happen if you shine a light in those corners? What do you want your life and work to look like? Why doesn't it look like that now? What can you do to propel it in that direction? These are powerful, attention-driving questions. See if you can think of more and write them in the back of the book. Go ahead; I won't be offended. It's by asking questions that we learn to focus our attention consciously on that which makes us better, smarter and happier.

By choosing where your attention goes, you choose the ideas that you will retain, and those will drive the next phase of your life. If they are inspirational and based in your calling, in your *why*, then you will be the chief pallbearer at the funeral of your former life. And it will be one hell of a wake.

Chapter 7

Reap The Possibilities

"Man is so made that when anything fires his soul, impossibilities vanish."

—JEAN DE LA FONTAINE, POET

Throughout our lives, there has always been a portion of our glass that appears empty. It's a portion that often screams for our attention. The news media primarily generates profit by focusing on this empty section. Yet it has always been our choice on where we place our focus. Our attention is ours. While it may at times take superhuman strength to focus on the portion of our glass that is full, focus we must, for until we focus on the full portion we will be less effective in our dealings with the portion that appears empty.

That is the power in reversing the course of the IRA wheel in order to put attention before retention. It lets you deploy your mind consciously rather than living on autopilot. It enables you to take charge of where your attention is spent rather than letting it go where the media wants it to go (usually to the negative). Most importantly, it empowers you to harness the power of your consciousness to improve your life today and in the future.

But the next logical question in the IRA-IAR model is this: if I'm supposed to be putting my attention on things that I want to retain and that will better me, what exactly are those things? Before I get into them, I want to take a closer look at the concept of attention and the lies that we tend to believe about self-improvement.

Pundits call self-improvement an "industry" for good reason: it's all about selling product.[27]Look at the books, tapes, CDs and workshops that the top gurus in the field sell and you can conclude one thing: the entire field is about shortcuts. It's enlightenment as a commodity. But do all the advice, programs and exercises really make any difference? Research suggests that for most people, they don't. And for the industry, that's the point. It's much more lucrative to sell someone a temporary high via a book or seminar and get them fired up by the idea that by simply buying the book or attending the seminar they are actually *making meaningful changes in their thinking.*

The truth is, they aren't. After a few days or weeks, the buzz fades. Behavior may have changed temporarily, but thinking didn't. So what do those people do in order to get back that illusory high? They buy more books, attend a weekend retreat, or even go on one of those $3,000 cruises where they can be bombarded with self-help messages and sales pitches with nowhere to run. What a racket.

There are many reasons why most self-improvement products do little or nothing for the people who consume them. Some are junk. Some are unrealistic. But for our discussion, the deeper reason that most programs fail is because they focus only on what and how instead of why. They try to get you to eat differently to lose weight instead of focusing on why you have a problem with food. They give you affirmations to help your self-esteem instead of looking at why you feel incapable and helpless in certain situations. Insert your favorite self-help brand here. It's the same dynamic: what and how questions suggest easy, relatively painless answers. Asking *why* opens the door to hard work and potentially painful revelations about our own role in our problems.

But why is the root of the tree. If you don't tend the root, the tree dies. So for any sort of advice to work, As Simon's Sinek's book title states it must start with why (and we're back to the book by Sinek!).[28] For change to be lasting, it can't be all about a temporary buzz that comes from some aphorisms in a book. It has to be about deep revelation and understanding of *why* you did things in the past and the purpose or calling—the *why*—that beckons to you in the future.

So my advice to you has nothing to do with a set program of materials and ideas. I've shared with you the IRA-IAR model because that's all about gaining conscious control over where you put your attention, but everything else is still uniquely yours. What you do with your attention will be completely different from what anyone else does with theirs—and that's where people say to me, "Steve, what do I do?"

Our cultural addiction to being told "read this, watch that, listen to this speech, follow these steps" is so strong, that even when we know we should break away from it, we have a hard time. Well, I'm not going to feed that addiction. My suggestion is all about choosing where your attention goes. After that, you can chart your course toward change for yourself. As long as you keep the *why* in front of you, any choice you make will be the right one.

WHERE TO PLACE YOUR ATTENTION

You are what you pay attention to. So in the course of building your life around the art of why, you should be changing your thinking by changing where your attention lands. That's where an approach I call RTP kicks in.

RTP stands for Reap The Possibilities. You reap what you sow, so you must sow possibilities in order to reap them. But that's just a phrase to help you remember the three behaviors that lie at the heart of this. Consciously and consistently put your attention on these three behaviors and over time, your thinking and circumstances will change. Here's what RTP really stands for:

1. **Read.** Harry Truman said, "Not all readers are leaders, but all leaders are readers." When you are trying to create a life of abundance, you must work from a place of abundance. You can't serve from an empty cup. You need to fill up your mind with riches. Odds are at least some of what you feed your mind right now is junk food. I consider anything to be junk food that reinforces the idea that life is to be feared, that you cannot do what you want to do, and that you need to buy or acquire to become someone important.

You are already someone important! You don't need to get or buy anything to be important. We have a nation built on scarcity. We are the richest nation on earth and yet the most impoverished in the way we think. So don't let the popular culture tell you where to put your attention—you decide where to put it! *Place your attention on that which you want to retain.*

In this journey to change, begin to consume written words that elevate you—mental health food, so to speak. Truly successful people who have balanced wealth and material success with family, wellness and community read challenging works that lift them up, task their minds and overturn their biases. When he was in office, President Theodore Roosevelt would consume books at a rate of one a day when busy and two to three when he had a free evening.[29] Of course, that was an era before radio, television, air travel and the Internet, so he had more time to read, but still—that's a volume of reading destined to fuel greatness.

When I wake up in the morning, the first things I see are books I have placed on the table next to my bed. I look at them before I do anything else or even—if I can—allow myself to *think* anything else. I'm devoted to letting the ideas within these books (they change over time, of course) shape my thinking over time, like raindrops over time can dissolve and shape stone. They are my *devotionals.*

What are your devotionals? What are the ideas you're letting into your mind through the written word? Live on the lifting; read that which elevates your spirit, reminds you of what's really important, and tells you the truth. Read that which insulates you against the lies and the negativity of a culture that's dedicated to making you feel that *you are not good enough*…but you could be if you had a new Lexus.

Some people argue that things you watch or listen to are just as good for shaping your thinking. I disagree. The trouble with audio or video is that there's a layer of mediation between you and the creator of the ideas. You have an announcer or a director and actors. But reading is a kind of telepathy. You read the words and hear them in your mind and bang!—it's you in conversation with Norman Vincent Peale or Plato or Jim Collins. There's nothing between you and the ideas. That's why reading is so powerful.

Read everything you can get your hands on as long as it's wise, elevated, and enlightened. Don't read things that buy into the scarcity economy, the fear-based manipulation of our culture. Read books on history, politics, economics, psychology and more. Read literary nonfiction, not the junk food that hogs the bookshelves and e-readers today. Read magazines from *Mother Jones* to *The Weekly Standard*. Read smart, well-written online magazines and blogs that challenge you, expose you to different viewpoints and open your eyes to things you had no idea about.

At the same time, purge your system of the garbage. Think of this time as a mental colon cleanse. Stop watching junk television. If you want to change your thinking and become a source of abundance, you should never set eyes on a Kardashian again. If you subscribe to junk celebrity magazines, cancel your subscriptions. Raise the quality, depth and intelligence of what you put into your mind and consume quality every single day. It will become a habit, and you'll gain new insight into your passion and purpose.

2. **Think.** My first book was called *Don't Believe Everything You Think*, and that's the motto I want you to adopt about your own mind. This is why you need to change what you see, hear and read. Where do you think your thinking comes from? So if you can't trust everything you see, hear and read, you can't trust everything you think. See, modern culture knows that the easiest way to manipulate you into spending money and being a passive non-participant in society is to activate your fear center. You're probably familiar with the acronym for FEAR: False Evidence Appearing Real.[30] Right? Fear lies to us. Fear distorts reality. Fear distorts what we believe about who we are and what we can accomplish.

For me, thinking means metacognition, which I defined earlier as being aware of how you think, of the patterns into which your mind tends to fall. Think of your brain as a hard but not impervious surface, like a wooden table. If you run a hard object over that surface in the same direction for years, it will eventually wear grooves in the wood. That's how your habitual thoughts work.

If you spend years living unconsciously and letting your attention fall on things related to fear and scarcity, then you will wear grooves in your brain, so to speak. In reality, the neural connections that carry certain thoughts become stronger the more you think those thoughts. After a while, those thoughts will dominate your thinking—you'll "slip into the grooves" easily, even automatically. That's why it's hard to change the way we think.

The power of metacognition is that we become conscious of our thought patterns and mental habits. And when we become conscious of something, we gain control over it. So one night you step back and catch yourself in the middle of fretting about not having a new car and you say, "Wait a sec, I'm feeling bad about myself because my car is three years old. That's crazy! I have a great wife, two great kids and a wonderful career. I'm not going to allow myself to be manipulated by marketing." Can you see how that kind of elevated cognition gives you the power to ignore ideas that bring you down and empowers you to refocus your attention on those that bear you up?

As I've said before, the majority likes to concentrate its thinking on what creates pleasure and security in the present, even if it's an illusion. Most people put their attention on things that a) give them brief pleasure, or b) things that assuage their existential terror about death, meaning, morality, and so on. It's the rare individual who can really look at the long view, the big picture, instead of obsessing about the minutiae of the moment. That's why political candidates spend so much time talking about amygdala-centric issues like abortion and birth control.

As you begin to change your thinking, you're going to find yourself part of a misunderstood minority: those who take the long view and who reject temporary pleasures in favor of long-term growth a wisdom. The majority won't understand you, but here's an incre' powerful idea to remember:

The majority is always wrong.

The sheep are led to the slaughter. The shepherd is in the minority, but he's the one leading the flock. The majority *thinks* it's right; that's how it gets to be the majority. But if you think about the greatest successes of our time—the inventors, entrepreneurs, artists and so on—nearly all have been ridiculed, mocked, scorned and made an outcast. That applies to great minds from Pablo Picasso[31] and Thomas Edison[32] to Steve Jobs[33] and Amazon.com's Jeff Bezos.[34] The majority always thinks geniuses are not only misinformed but also dangerous—and the majority is almost always wrong. In fact, if someone ever calls one of your ideas "insane," you might want to start thinking about how you're going to spend all the money you're going to make!

The majority is wrong in its thinking because the majority of human beings are limited by their brains. We're all human, and we all face the same limitations. But some people work past those limitations and learn to focus their attention away from bread, circuses and reality TV. Who defines what the right mind is? You do, for yourself. Being in a state of metacognition is about seeing the truth about the lies you may have been telling yourself. Think about the word *rationalize*, which means to make excuses for ill-advised thoughts or actions. Did it ever occur to you that to rationalize means to tell yourself *rational lies*?

It's time for you to begin reminding yourself to step back and watch yourself think. Ask yourself why you think the way you do. Ask yourself why certain events or statements trigger certain types of behavior in you. Ask why you behaved the way you did in a certain situation. Take ownership. Don't blame. Blame disempowers you; it's the ego's way of skirting responsibility. Own your choices and be empowered to make different ones in the future.

 the question, "What was I afraid of?" Often our most unat-

ers are linked to emotional fears. Start learning to con-

thinking away from habitual, ingrained patterns

d replace them with hope, possibility and courage.

You'll start cutting new grooves in your brain and creating new cognitive habits.

I suggest using something to remind you to do this. Unconscious thinking creeps up on us; it's important to have some sort of touchstone or artifact to prompt you to catch unhealthy thinking while it's happening. It might be a small stone or special coin in your pocket, a bracelet that one of your kids made in school, a reminder card that you keep on the sun visor in your car, or the wallpaper of your smart phone. Doesn't matter. Sprinkle multiple reminders to "think different" throughout your life. Don't leave this to chance.

3. **Partner.** You can do this alone...maybe. But it's not likely. And why would you want to? Great leaders allow themselves to be led. Partnering is all about acknowledging a simple, universal truth: change is *hard*. When you leave old attitudes behind, chase a new calling, or exorcise negative people from your space, you're presiding over the death of something. We've already discussed how much anxiety that causes us. So we resist. Remember, IRA also stands for Individual Resistance Account. We backslide, we make excuses, we cheat. It's common and human, but it also destroys our progress.

Partners help you establish your new patterns when you enter into a relationship of accountability. We can delude ourselves; self-delusion, not money, is the root of all evil. But it's much more difficult to get away with deceiving another person who we've charged with assisting us in keeping the promises we make. It's a binary situation: either you're doing what you said you would, or you aren't. If you aren't, a partner is the one who taps you on the shoulder, points the way to the gym or counselor's office or whatever you have committed yourself to be doing.

You can see how serious someone is about changing their thinking and behavior based on how accountable they make themselves to others. It's nothing to say, "I'm going to get my debt under control this year." It costs you nothing and there's nothing to hold you to any sort of plan. It's a different story when the same person says, "I'm going to get my debt under control this year. I have an appointment with a financial advisor on Thursday."

That's an instant accountability structure. Partnering is not about someone showing you what to do; you already know how to save money and not use your credit cards. It's about someone getting you to do what you know you should do. It's about having someone (or multiple some-ones) who helps you overcome the tidal pull of the amygdala and not give in to those voices that say *You're not good enough, you can't do this, you need to buy something to make yourself feel better.*

Whom can you partner with? How about a personal trainer, a financial advisor or a marriage counselor? How about a friend, pastor or your spouse? How about your boss, a co-worker or a close friend? Anyone can be a partner as long as you give him or her permission to keep you accountable to your goals, and as long as he or she is willing to call you out when you get lazy or fall into self-deception.

There's another important principle at work here as well. As an enlightened person with metacognition and conscious attention, you become a leader. Those who have the will and wisdom to transform their lives become beacons for others who are trying to do the same. Truly successful people do what unsuccessful people are un*will*ing to do. Transformation is an act of *will*. When you emerge from this time of change, you'll become a leader.

But leaders don't lead by command. They lead by who they are. Foster Mobley, a brilliant leadership coach and thinker, says, "Leaders go first." You can't lead others by what you say. You lead others by being the change you wish to see in the world—by being a living example of the power of directed attention and self-awareness. The people you choose to partner with are leaders, too. Otherwise, you wouldn't choose them. We choose those stronger than ourselves to lift us up. A person who's never sacrificed for the big picture or finished anything in his life is not going to inspire anyone to work hard.

As you move through this time of immense change, where you're beginning to fill your head with new reading and learning to watch your own thoughts in action, also start reaching out to partners. They are probably all around you—people with the love, honesty and humility to know that we all need help. We are all weak and sometimes the greatest strength lies in acknowledging this, reaching out and saying, "Guide me."

Ulysses was not a great explorer because of his bravery, but because of his humility. When other sailors had encountered singing of the Sirens, they said, "I can handle that." Then they heard the songs and dashed their ships to pieces on the rocks. But Ulysses said, "...take me and bind me to the crosspiece half way up the mast..." In doing so, he saved himself and his crew. Don't be afraid to ask for help. Find wise partners who understand the journey you're on.

In the end, RTP is about getting your head on straight. You must have your head on straight to see straight. There's a line in the Bible that says Heaven is for those who place their hands to the plow and don't look back. Our rows won't be straight if we keep looking back. Keep your hands on the plow and you'll reap the possibilities.

Chapter 8

ANGEL'S ADVOCATE

*Optimism is the faith that leads to achievement. Nothing
can be done without hope and confidence.*

—HELEN KELLER

In the book *Stumbling on Happiness,*[35] Daniel Gilbert wrote that we have an psychological internal immune system that allows us to overcome the big challenges in life. Some parts of that immune system include finding a more positive view, growing through difficult experiences and finding blessings even in hard times. There's an old saying that goes, "It's an ill wind that blows nobody (any) good." Meaning, it's very rare that something happens that's so bad that it doesn't also contain blessings in it as well as pain. Sometimes the blessings are hard to see, or they take time to show themselves. I think you would have had a hard time finding people in New Orleans to insist that Hurricane Katrina was a blessing, but over the long term it's yielded some positive changes for the city, including a rebirth of some decaying areas and a better flood-protection infrastructure.[36]

We're wired to find growth and strength in hard times. That's part of building self-efficacy. Human beings don't do well with too much comfort and complacency; we crave challenge. Why else do successful lawyers and doctors leave careers of exceptional success and financial reward to start cafes or become travel writers? Why do millionaire entrepreneurs sell their companies and start new ones from scratch? We crave difficulty. We love to test ourselves against the universal forces of *You can't* and *It's not possible.*

In his book, Gilbert also wrote that what is more troubling for humans is when we don't take our big chances and have to live with the regret of what might have been. That's true. He also said that with the big challenges, we learn no matter what the outcome is and are wiser and better for it. It's the little, day-to-day irritations that bring unhappiness. They don't engage our internal psychological immune system.[37] Instead, I see them nibbling away at us like black flies, so its better in the long run to take on bigger challenges and learn to not sweat the small stuff.

It appears that people who have wired their brains to be more resilient during bad times enjoy a more robust immune system than those who are more likely to adhere to Seligman and Maier's "learned helplessness" as mentioned in Chapter 1.[38] So thinking positive and believing that we can overcome anything is key to not only a more successful life but a richer, healthier quality of life as well.

YOUR FULL CUP

As we draw near to the end of our time together, I want to bring your attention—your consciously controlled attention—to two states of being that I believe will make it impossible for you NOT to passionately pursue the use of the tools I've laid out for you. The first is *gratitude.* I would argue that gratitude, not happiness, is the ultimate goal state of every healthy human being on this earth. Why? Because happiness is transitory. I can feel happy when I eat a great piece of gourmet dark chocolate, but that happiness doesn't change who I am. It's not a product of an expanded awareness and perspective.

But when I become grateful for that chocolate, my awareness shifts. I become grateful for the people who made it. I become grateful for the farmers who grew the cocoa beans and that I have enough money to afford to pay for a delicacy that many in the world will never be able to afford. My perspective grows larger, as does my humility. Gratitude makes me a citizen of a wider world.

Thanksgiving may be the most important holiday of the year, especially with all that is going on in the world today. Today, I believe a spirit of gratitude is needed more than ever. I once read that it is impossible to be thankful and to also be depressed. Happiness and gratitude are inextricably linked. Wouldn't it also stand to reason that unhappiness is linked to ungratefulness? Clearly it takes strength, courage and effort to prime the spirit of gratitude, especially when in the present, life might be difficult, painful, violent or seemingly without hope. All I can say is "Try harder."

We are rich beyond belief, no matter what trials or adversity stand in our way. These trials are best addressed not by focusing on what's missing, but on what is present. If you have oxygen in your lungs – if you are alive – you have cause for gratitude. As the saying goes, "Any day above ground is a good day." Elderly people often say this because they have come to truly appreciate the simple things in life even as they watch friends die. Being intimate with death makes one genuinely appreciate how marvelous life is despite all the small, trivial setbacks.

You are called to serve others, not only yourself. How are you to serve from an empty cup? You can't. Let me tell you, if you believe that your cup is empty, you will run around at a ridiculous pace doing anything to fill your cup, even when it doesn't really need filling! Instead, you should be appreciating how full your cup is and filling the cups of others. Treat your cup like a coffee mug. When you pour too much water into it, it overflows. That water then runs into the cups of others, making them aware of how many gifts they possess. When we realize how full our lives truly are—giving becomes easy. We will give of our time, we will give of our money and we will give of our lives. I have found this to be the only way to live a life that is rich, passionate and filled with joy.

WRITE YOUR GRATITUDE LIST

Aldous Huxley said, "Most human beings have an almost infinite capacity for taking things for granted." I want you to defy that tendency and write your Gratitude List.

I doubt if very many people in our nation have a Gratitude List. Your mind and our culture will convince you not to do it. They'll whisper, "You deserve everything you have." And maybe you do, but that's no reason to take it for granted. Because when you do, you're more likely to become someone from whom everything can easily be taken away. Sustainable good fortune demands sustained gratitude.

Take out a pen and paper right now and start writing your list. It's the most powerful tool in your toolbox for personal transformation. It will move you faster than anything from IRA thinking to IAR thinking. Within minutes, focusing on gratitude changes your mind. That's why the most successful people I know have hundreds of things on their Gratitude List. I know one man, the most successful person I know, who has one thousand items on his list.

What's on your list? How about the most elemental things of all? Write, *I can walk. I can talk. I can think. I can see. I can hear. I have my teeth. I have food to eat. I have clean water to drink.* Clean water is something that is not available to 1.1 billion human beings on the planet,[39] one fourth of the world's population. You have a room in your house where you can walk in and with the touch of a lever, create a personal waterfall of clean water that you're not even drinking. Nine thousand people today will die from hunger. I'm not trying to attach guilt here, just perspective. This isn't about feeling guilty; it's about feeling grateful that you won't die from hunger because you have access to good food.

Gratitude, in the end, is about understanding that there is very little that separates us from those who don't have what we have. Often, it's not something inherent like talent. There are people with more natural talent than you for medicine, law or business who are living in squalor in Mumbai slums. Sometimes, it's only a blend of luck, good upbringing, and the right social connection that makes the difference between a CEO and a beggar. The difference is so small!

Did you ever stop to think that when you're driving at high speed on a two-lane highway with no median that you're one inch from death at all times? If you turn that wheel just an inch to the left, you'll be obliterated by oncoming traffic. Life is that tenuous, and that's what makes it precious. In his book *Watership Down*, Richard Adams said, "Many human beings say that they enjoy the winter, but what they really enjoy is feeling proof against it." Gratitude is the full awareness that we are lucky to be driving straight and not pulling into oncoming traffic, that we have thick windows and a furnace against the snows of winter, being aware that others don't have the same blessings…and developing a mindset to serve those who are not as fortunate as we.

It is impossible to feel entitled and live in a state of thankfulness. With thankfulness, you have a full cup and instead of working to fill your own cup with money and position, you work to fill other people's cups. You are rich beyond belief. Change your comparisons. How can you be a source of abundance if you don't sense your own? Write your list. Fill it with things that you might otherwise not think twice about: your spouse, your kids, your home, your friends, your health. Then move on to material possessions or achievements. Try to add something new every day until your list is impossibly long. Then keep adding to it.

WHY PLAY DEVIL'S ADVOCATE?

In my industry, financial services, I have a saying: "Planners who plan for the worst are the worst planners." This goes back to the idea that worry and pessimism are signs of a mature mind when in reality they are signs of low self-efficacy. Besides gratitude, the other key state of mind I want you to cultivate is *optimism*. I don't mean blind optimism that denies reality. But I do mean confident optimism that says:

Sometimes the worst happens. If it does, I can handle it.
Sometimes the best happens. If it
does, I will appreciate it.

You can't fear the worst and serve anyone, including yourself. The great ship captain is aware of the storm, but he doesn't dwell on the storm. He's prepared for it, but he doesn't assume that the ship will sink. That's setting yourself up for defeat. Hope is not a success strategy.

Finish this statement: "Hope for the best…" Plan for the worst, right? That's the Devil's Advocate. We know it because we love to play it. We love to spin out the worst case scenario and give our anxiety free rein to run wild. It happens all the time in financial planning. A client will say, "Okay, what's the worst thing that could happen?" But have you ever heard anyone say, "Hey, can we play Angel's Advocate and talk about the best thing that could happen?" I doubt it. But why not? The best-case scenario does come to pass from time to time, you know. But we don't look at it for fear of seeming blindly optimistic and being disappointed.

Imagine taking a cruise. You approach the captain and ask, "So, Captain, what's the plan?" He says, "Oh, it's a big ocean. We plan to sink. But we have some beautiful lifeboats!" What kind of captain says that? Not one who's in the profession very long. If you plan only for the worst, then you have nothing in your toolbox when the best comes to pass. Plan A cannot be the lifeboat; Plan A must be the ship not sinking. Our culture considers pessimism to be realism, but nothing in history supports the pessimistic view.

Rather than play Devil's Advocate, I want you to retrain your brain to play Angel's Advocate. Catch yourself beginning to focus on the worst that could happen and instead, redirect your thinking to the best that could happen. The new phrase that captures this is, "Plan for the best, prepare for the worst." When the storm is coming, it's prudent to lay in supplies, stock up on firewood, batteries and blankets and board up the windows. But it doesn't make sense to live every day in terror that your house is about to be washed into the ocean.

Is it possible that you'll go to your annual physical and find out you have cancer? Of course. But is it likely to happen? No. What's more likely is that you'll find out you're in pretty good health. Just because our fears are possible, that doesn't mean they are probable. When it comes to your fears, don't believe everything you think. Don't forget that when it comes to your own life, you lack two vital qualities: objectivity and perspective. You hire a lawyer, physician or financial planner to lend you objectivity and perspective born of professional experience.

The best does happen...every day. Think on the best that can happen and you increase the odds that it will happen. This will fuel your optimism.

Gratitude and optimism are two sides of the same coin. The objects of your gratitude are proof that the best things DO happen. Did you ever stop to think of that? This is the point—to stop and think. The fact that you have so much to be grateful for is evidence that positive thinking is warranted. To retune your thinking, try changing what you say to others and yourself. When you get up in the morning, tell yourself out loud that it's going to be a fantastic day. When someone asks you how you are, say, "I'm so good I can't stand it." You really will be that good if you've been reading your gratitude list and are grateful.

When someone else starts talking about the worst-case outcome, parry that energy by talking about the good that could happen. The more you do this, the more that self-talk will "infect" your mind with optimism and hope.

MAN ON THE MOON

I get some push back on this idea. Some people say to me, "Steve, bad things do happen. If you don't plan for them, how can you be prepared?" I never said not to be prepared. That's why we have insurance. Nobody ever bought insurance hoping to get sick or get in a car accident. We buy it because we acknowledge that things do happen. But we don't base our lives on that possibility. So keep the earthquake kit in your basement. Keep the first aid kit in the car. But never forget that in the big picture, optimism is justified.

If you want proof, look no further than the most audacious episode in modern human history: the push to put men on the moon. In 1961, "President John F. Kennedy made the bold, public claim that the U.S would land a man on the moon before the end of the decade," but nothing remotely so complex had ever been attempted. By 1960, we'd had the Mercury space program immortalized in *The Right Stuff*, but putting an astronaut into the earth's orbit is child's play compared with the physics, engineering, computer science and aeronautics challenges of sending men to the moon, 238,900 miles away.

Yet we, and the then-USSR, began the infamous space race, both countries spending billions of dollars and using the best minds in the world to first identify the obstacles to landing on the moon and then to solve them. Elaborate development, testing and launch facilities were built, changing the very character of south Florida and Houston, Texas. New engineering ideas were tried. Pilots were subjected to physical and psychological testing that was, in many cases, invented on the fly. The whole enterprise had a pell-mell, Rube Goldberg quality to it—frantic engineers goaded on by even more frantic politicians to do the impossible.

It shouldn't have worked. The level of engineering needed to launch a craft into an earth-moon transit, manage a safe descent to the lunar surface, keep life support going for multiple pilots, safely reunite the lunar and command modules, and return the entire awkward machine home is staggeringly complex. Odds are if the people involved had allowed themselves to think about the worst-case scenario, they would have frozen in place. The worst-case scenario, after all, was pretty terrible: screaming astronauts burning up on re-entry or stranded forever on the moon's surface, a nation humiliated, billions wasted. With the risks at hand, there was every reason to think pessimistically, play it safe, and plan for the worst.

But they didn't. NASA and its people turned their brilliant minds to how problems could be solved and assumed that, yes, this incredible goal could be reached. They prepared for the worst with backup systems and safety technology, but they forged ahead toward the best outcome, creating a new era as they went. And of course, after many preparatory flights and one tragedy—the loss of Apollo 1 and its crew in a 1961 launch pad fire—the U.S. succeeded in landing men on the moon in 1969.[40] We also went back again and again for years.

Even when we failed, we succeeded. Take the famous Apollo 13 mission, immortalized by the movie starring Tom Hanks. That mission to the moon was ruined by an explosion in the spacecraft's fuel system, putting the lives of astronauts Jim Lovell, Fred Haise and Jack Swigert in mortal danger. It was widely presumed that with the capsule's wrecked life support system, damaged navigation and limited oxygen, the trio would never make it back to earth.

But they did. Again, there was no defeat in the attitudes of the team at Mission Control or the three astronauts. Pessimism would have been the logical stance given the facts on the ground. But nobody went there. Everyone assumed that there was hope and so they created hope. In the end, as you know, the can-do spirit of the people involved and their ingenuity turned what could have been the darkest hour in the history of the space program into one of its finest.

Pessimism aids nothing. It helps no one. Playing the Devil's Advocate is an intellectual game designed to relieve us of the responsibility for making the best happen. If we assume that the best outcome is out of reach, then we don't have to work to bring it about. We can choose lazily and plan for the worst, and when it happens, exclaim, "See? I told you!"

Optimism takes bravery and work. But it's the path of the angels. Cultivate gratitude and optimism and you will discover how far they can take you.

Chapter 9

Your Calling

"Every calling is great when greatly pursued."

—Oliver Wendell Holmes

Tom Dawkins, an Australian social entrepreneur and co-founder of the social funding website StartSomeGood.com, recently shared the story of finding his calling on the blog WhatsYourCalling.org. I share some of it with you as a way of getting this conversation started:

"...But it was in San Francisco, not Spokane, that I found my calling. I was invited to attend the State of the World Forum, held in San Francisco in 1995. It was a post–Cold War pow-wow designed to build consensus on the challenges and opportunities facing the world. Participants included Mikael Gorbachev, Margaret Thatcher, Ronald Reagan, Ted Turner, Thich Nhat Hanh, Richard Leakey, Jane Goodall, Rigoberta Menchu Tum and numerous other Nobel Laureattes, business people, environmentalists, authors, thinkers and politicians.

...It was a heady, extraordinary experience. The first day we arrived we were told that we represented '2 billion young people.' We participated in dialogue's with Nobel Peace Prize winners, world leaders (including Gorbachev and then Vice-President

later President of South Africa Thabo Mbeki), representatives from the UN and other global organizations and, of course, with each other. During the week I was there I slept for only a few hours a night and barely ate. I wasn't hungry, I wasn't tired. I was infatuated with a newfound sensation of being included in conversation that, it seemed, really mattered. Being listened to and told my opinions mattered. I felt, in a word, empowered.

"But as I left the Forum this feeling of empowerment was balanced with another sensation: dissatisfaction. This can't be good enough I thought to myself. If we are serious about including the perspectives of young people in conversation that matter, and we must be, then it can't be based on pretending that a group of upper-middle class kids who already have the opportunity to be in America (just happening to be in the right time at the right place) 'represent' the young people of the world. I felt intensely, immediately, that we needed to build better, more genuinely representative platforms and opportunities for young people from diverse perspectives to share their stories, and that this could never truly happen inside the closed rooms of conferences.

In dissatisfaction we can sometimes find our calling: something that needs changing about the world, and the determination that it must be us to change it. This is not the only type of calling of course, but for me it was the cause I had been looking for, the focus I needed, the work that needed doing.

Since then I have been working to allow more people's voices to be heard, to build a more democratic society and world. First my focus was on young people and event-based, founding organizations at high school and university which hosted a variety of conferences, debates and arts gatherings. In 2000 I realized that the Internet was the platform I had been looking for, and media the marketplace of ideas in our society, and founded Vibewire, an organization that continues to create opportunities for political and creative expression for young Australians. Then two years at Ashoka exploring how social media could help create an Everyone a Changemaker world, one where all voices and perspectives can be heard, and more recently co-founding StartSomeGood.com, a platform for Changemakers to access the resources and support they need to turn their ideas into action and impact.

For me this is what I want to do with the rest of my life, to help communities and individuals rise to the challenges that confront us and in so doing create a more equitable, sustainable and just world, one based on democratic participation and individual empowerment.

I know from my journey that a calling, or a cause, can arise at any moment, as a result of the stories you see, hear, experience and share. They can be grandiose (like mine), or humble, community-focused or individualistic, a life-long pursuit or a chapter amongst many. All are equally valid; all share an essential spark of human creativity, idealism and imagination. If you are still looking for a calling I would simply advise: stay open. Open minded, open hearted and, simply, open-eyed. Possibility, opportunity, challenges and tragedy are all around us. The world is both an amazing and a difficult place and is made better by each person who brings their whole self into it and finds a way to do work which inspires and fulfills them..."

I don't know about you, but I envy Tom Dawkins. Finding that kind of passionate calling so young is amazing (he was the equivalent of a high school senior when he went to the forum). But that's the power of a calling: it can transform your life in an instant and fill you with such energy that you will barely be able to keep your feet on the ground. As we move into the final chapter of this brief book, I want to talk about the nature of the calling and remind you, in case you have forgotten, that there is a calling waiting for you if you have the courage to let it in.

THE END POINT

The monk, writer and mystic Thomas Merton wrote, "...if you want to identify me, ask me not where I live, or what I like to eat, or how I comb my hair, but ask me what I think I am living for, in detail, and ask me what I think is keeping me from living fully for the thing I want to live for." That's the question I hope you will ask yourself after digging deeply into the stuff of the last few chapters. After you engage in the multi-step process to begin changing your behavior...after you turn your IRA into an IAR and consciously control where your attention lands... after you begin to Read, Think and Partner, and after you write your Gratitude List, what's left? What's left is your *calling.*

The calling is the end point of this entire process. It's also the beginning. It's the end because after you have truly opened your eyes, accepted your failures, transformed your thinking and attention, and developed your thankfulness and optimism muscles, there's no going back. Your old life is dead. What lies before you will be different, even if nothing changes outwardly.

What do I mean by that? I mean that even if you continue to do the same job and live in the same community, you will carry out your job and relate to the community in completely different ways. There aren't many options here: either you will continue to do what you have been doing but with markedly different goals, intentions and results, or you will overthrow your previous life and move into something completely different. There is no right or wrong choice; what matters is that you acknowledge that there is no going back and take your new wisdom and awareness and move forward. Bury your old way of living—cremate it, do whatever you need to do to leave it behind—then don't look back.

Finding your calling is the death of your old life because we are fueled by our sense of priorities. All priorities stem from the fact of mortality; we worry that we won't have time to accomplish what we want before we decay and die. It's that raw and real. When you're immersed in a fear (False Evidence Appearing Real) mentality, you're only concerned about getting, grabbing and grasping. Fear, greed and envy empty your cup and you'll spend all your time trying to fill it before it's too late. When you discover these new ways of thinking and being, your priorities *cannot* remain the same. Whatever you served when you were thinking only about your fear—when you were running away from whatever you felt was chasing you—will be impossible to serve in your new state.

That means you will have some choices to make. The first and most elemental is a choice I think you'll have an easy time making: *do I pay attention to the new voices speaking to me?* Of course you do. I don't think you'll have a choice. Few people open their eyes to what life can truly become and choose to ignore the possibilities before them.

The second choice is *what to do next?* That's where the concept of the calling comes into play. With the new sense of possibility filling your mind, you'll almost certainly find yourself gravitating to new paths, or perhaps old paths that you almost followed years before but turned away from. After your transformation begins, the time to open your mind to your calling arrives. That's why this is the end. But it's also the beginning of a new era.

THE BEGINNING

This is also the beginning because you will approach everything you do from the perspective of your new, conscious thinking. The day that gratitude is a natural part of your life, that you automatically choose where to place your attention, that you reject short-term pleasure in favor of long-term growth—that's the first inning of your new ballgame.

When you reach this point, you will probably find yourself confronted by a lot of new feelings and questions, including

-   How can I keep going in my old career?
-   What should my priorities be now?
-   Whom should I associate with?
-   Whom and what should I get out of my life?
-   What do I do with the next decade?
-   How do I give my life meaning?

Those are unnerving, wonderful questions. I suggest you not only ask them, but embrace them in all their complexity. This is the time to ask tough questions and come up with answers that may not satisfy everyone. The fact is, when you shift your consciousness and begin living your life based on why, you'll tick some folks off. People who have given themselves over body and soul to the empty pursuit of material things tend to react with anger when someone else's truer success reveals them as the benighted souls they are. Not everyone will be happy for your new path, so don't expect it. The people who love and need you will be thrilled.

The beginning of things means you have the chance to take that fork in the road. It's time to go after your calling, the thing that makes life worth living. Haven't you waited long enough?

THE CALLING

But what is a calling? For starters, it's not some vaguely religious imperative that leads you to a silent life in a Trappist monastery. That's the right path for a select few, but probably not for you. No, the calling is the thing that you feel, down deep, you were put on this earth to do. It's the pursuit that gives your life zest and joy and that fires your passions. It's the thing you could and would do for days with little sleep and no food, never feeling tired or hungry.

Put simply, your calling is the thing that turns you from someone who serves only yourself into someone who serves as many people as possible. You don't have to consciously say, "I will now serve thousands of people." It happens automatically, as a sort of side effect of being in your calling. The calling, by its nature, radiates enlightenment, compassion or aid. Have you ever noticed that people who overthrow previous lives in business or finance to engage in social justice or charity rarely do anything for themselves? It's always about others. The person with the calling sees some benefits as well, but as a result of bringing blessings to others—of being the change.

You are called to be someone greater than who you are being today. If you are living a life that feels laid out for you by someone else, or you feel drained and emptied by the demands of our society, you are ignoring the call. The concept of the calling derives from the Latin *vocare*,[41] which means "to call," and is sometimes interchangeable with the word "vocation." The Catholic Church used the word "vocation" specifically to refer to a special calling to the religious life, as a priest, monk or nun. Martin Luther expanded the meaning of the word to apply to secular work that serves others.

It doesn't matter whether you are a religious believer or not. When it comes to your calling, it doesn't matter whether you believe each of us has a destined occupation or if we are simply random bits of matter in a meaningless universe. What does matter are three facts:

1. You are here. You have the privilege to exist for this moment.
2. You have the potential to be an agent of positive change in the world.
3. You are probably feeling a sense of dissatisfaction with the path you are on.

That dissatisfaction comes from the incongruity that I mentioned early in the book. You see, we are all made to follow an ideal path doing something and being someone that speaks to our deepest selves. For some of us, that means being a banker or an accountant. For others, it means being an actor or a volunteer firefighter. For still others it has nothing to do with an occupation—they might work as a middle manager but have a calling to write poetry or build wooden boats on the weekends. But a calling is a compulsion that moves you toward a new future...when you finally allow yourself to feel and recognize it.

The entire process I've laid out in this book is all about opening yourself up to your calling. When you are buried up to your neck in a fear-based personal economy, chasing after things that can never fill you up, you can't even acknowledge that your calling exists. Maybe you don't recognize it because you're running too fast to get away from the lion that's chasing you. Maybe you don't want to recognize it because you turned your back on it when you were younger in favor of a "safe" path that pleased your parents or promised you a lot of money. Either way, you're blind to your calling.

By following the advice I've outlined in these pages, you'll open your eyes. You won't see or accept your calling until you live consciously and find your gratitude and perspective on life. When you do, your calling should become as obvious as the sun in the sky.

WHAT'S YOUR CALLING?

Let me be clear about something: having a calling does not mean you have to quit your job and become an impoverished guitar player roaming the back streets of America with your family in a trailer. But you could. Seriously, it's about knowing what path is most perfectly suited to your mind, your heart and your spirit, then following it in the way that brings you and others the greatest blessings. For some, that will be giving up everything about their old lives and going in a completely new direction. For them, there's no going back, but I think that's a bit extreme.

A more prudent approach is to choose a destination, chart out a path to get there, and start becoming a new person inside immediately. That way, you get to keep your house, and your friends and family don't threaten to have you committed, which is a plus. Over time, you might decide that with your new graduate degree or previously unknown talent for gourmet cooking that it's time to quit your job, move to the city, start your own restaurant or become a political activist. Who knows? Finding your calling means listening, perhaps for the first time, to the voice inside you that says, "That way. Take that road." It's a road you've driven by a million times in your life but never gone down. Heeding your calling means turning down that road. You can keep going and never come back, or you can drive for a few miles, turn around, and decide to come back for more exploring another day.

So following your calling doesn't have to be extreme. But it does have to be a complete commitment on your part. That should not be difficult, because you will have already made irrevocable changes to your thinking. The important thing is making progress, moving down that road and not giving in to the temptation to go back to the way things were. Trust me, there will be temptations, usually involving material comforts and wealth but also involving selling out the ideals you have come to cherish. That's where that long-term thinking comes in. With your calling in hand, you can have a true vision for your life. You can have purpose. That's more important than anything else.

So how do you find your calling? You don't. It finds you. It's already in you. It's been there since you were old enough to grasp the idea that people were different things. Some were writers. Some were cops. Some were gardeners. Some were pilots. Some were speakers. I ignored my calling for years, as I told you. I was so concerned with being wholesaler of the year that I turned a deaf ear to my passion, which was speaking. It was only after my marriage crisis and my new awareness of the legacy of my father's abandonment that I realized what really got me fired up was speaking to audiences about the topics in this book.

When I fully embraced that, my speaking career came to me. It didn't matter that I didn't have a doctorate. It didn't matter that I wasn't a celebrity. It didn't matter when I started that I hadn't written a book. Passion did all the speaking for me. People felt the fire I had burning in me to bring my message and booked me with a frequency that was, and is, gratifying.

So how do you find your calling? Start by looking within yourself. Find that still, small voice that's been speaking to you for years when things in your career or life became rough or discouraging. What alternate path has it asked you to consider? Your calling has always been within you, and now is the time to listen to it. Ask yourself what you have always thought of doing, if only you could make enough money to live on. Ask yourself how you could take your current career and turn it upside down to serve your passion. Ask yourself what you can do to fully become the person you know you can be—the highest, best version of yourself in every way.

That's not about money, position or influence. That's about service, love, hope and gratitude. It's about becoming the blessing that you bring to others. Discovering and living your calling is about knowing *why*. Your calling is why you were put on this earth.

It doesn't matter if you work as a financial advisor, teacher, meter maid, construction worker or city councilperson. There is a world-changer within you. It's always been there. Using the tools I've given you, I bet you can find it.

Go on. Prove me right. And remember the wise words of the British lawyer Louis Nizer:

> *"A man who works with his hands is a laborer;*
> *a man who works with his hands and his brain is a craftsman;*
> *but a man who works with his hands and his brain and his heart is an artist."*

End Notes

1. *Sales by Product 1995-2013.*: Jackson National Life Insurance

2. "Extreme Weather and Climate Change: The Southwest | Climate Central."*Extreme Weather and Climate Change: The Southwest | Climate Central.* Climate Central, 16 Nov. 2011.

3. Seligman, M.E.P.; Maier, S.F. (1967). "Failure to escape traumatic shock," *Journal of Experimental Psychology* 74: 1–9.

4. Seligman, Martin. *Learned Optimism.* New York, NY: Pocket Books, 1998.

5. Seligman, Martin. *Learned Optimism.* New York, NY: Pocket Books, 1998.

6. Koppel, Robert. *The Intuitive Trader: Developing Your Inner Trading Wisdom for More Successful Trades.* New York: John Wiley, 1996

7. Sinek, Simon. *Start with Why: How Great Leaders Get Everyone to Take Action.* New York: Portfolio, 2009.

8. Collins, James C. *How the Mighty Fall: and Why Some Companies Never Give In.* New York: Collins Business, 2009.

9. Joe Pavlish, "A Life Lost in Sin City," *Montana Kaimin,* January 28, 2011.

10. Collins, James. *Good to great: Why some companies make the leap--and others don't.* New York, NY: HarperBusiness, 2001.

11. Cassara, Lou. *From Selling to Serving: The Essence of Client Creation.* Chicago, IL: Dearborn Trade Publishing, 2004.

12. "Corpus+callosum." *The Free Dictionary.* Farlex

13. Churchland, P.M. (1981) *Eliminative Materialism and the Propositional Attitudes.* Journal of Philosophy 78(2): 67-90.

14. Barabási, Albert-László. *Linked: How Everything Is Connected to Everything Else and What It Means for Business, Science, and Everyday Life.* New York: Plume, 2003.

15. "Miami Property Market Booming: Yet Still Offers Value for Money." *A Place in the Sun.*

16. Das, Karnamrita. "Searching for Our Authentic Story-The Holy Grail of the Seekers Quest." *Krishna.com.* 2012

17. "Definition of Hubris." *Dictionary.com.* Dictionary.com

18. Wolff, Richard. *Capitalism Hits the Fan: The Global Economic Meltdown and What to Do About It.* Northhampton, MA: Olive Branch Press, 2009.

19. Fraser, Emily. "Start Your Best Year Yet with Reflection and Release." *Women Communicators of Austin.* Jan. 2014

20. Norcross, J. C., Mrykalo, M. S. and Blagys, M. D. (2002), *Auld lang Syne*: *Success predictors, change processes, and self-reported outcomes of New Year's resolvers and nonresolvers.* J. Clin. Psychol., 58: 397–405. doi: 10.1002/jclp.1151

21. Hall, Roger. "Stress Refresher For Food Science Leaders" (PowerPoint presentation). 2006.

22. Gottlieb, Lori. "How to Land Your Kid in Therapy," *The Atlantic Monthly*, July 2011.

23. Lester, Jason, *Running on Faith: The Principles, Passion and Pursuit of a Winning Life.* New York, NY: HarperOne, 2010.

24. Tolstoy, Leo. "Three Questions." *The Literature Network*

25. *Thinking, Fast and Slow by Daniel Kahneman*. S.l.: Garamond, 2012

26. Hooper, Richard, *Jesus, Buddha, Krishna & Lao Tzu: The Parallel Sayings*. Newburyport, MA: Hampton Roads Publishing, 2012.

27. Taylor, Jim. "Personal Growth: Is the Self-help Industry a Fraud?" *Psychology Today: Health, Help, Happiness + Find a Therapist*. April 18, 2011.

28. Sinek, Simon. *Start with Why: How Great Leaders Get Everyone to Take Action*. New York: Portfolio, 2009.

29. Chilton, Martin. "President Obama's Reading Habits." *The Telegraph*. Telegraph Media Group, 23 Jan, 2012

30. Montgomery, Joanna. "False Evidence Appearing Real." *The Huffington Post*. TheHuffingtonPost.com, 13 May 2013

31. "Pablo Picasso." *Wikipedia*. Wikimedia Foundation, 16 Aug. 2014

32. Giang, Alana Horowitz and Vivian. "17 People Who Were Fired Before They Became Rich And Famous." *Business Insider*. Business Insider, Inc, 31 Mar. 2012.

33. Siegel, Joel. "When Steve Jobs Got Fired By Apple." *ABC News*. ABC News Network, 06 Oct. 2011.

34. Appelo, Tim. "10 Things You Didn't Know About Jeff Bezos and Amazon - Hollywood Reporter." *The Hollywood Reporter*. 18 Oct. 2013

35. Gilbert, Daniel Todd. Stumbling on Happiness. New York, NY: Vintage Books, 2007.

36. "Completion of New Orleans' 100-year Flood Protection System Is a Significant Recovery Milestone: An Editorial." *NOLA.com*. The Times-Picayune, 29 May 2011

37. Gilbert, Daniel Todd. Stumbling on Happiness. New York, NY: Vintage Books, 2007.

38. Seligman, M.E.P.; Maier, S.F. (1967). "Failure to escape traumatic shock," *Journal of Experimental Psychology* 74: 1–9.

39. "Health through Safe Drinking Water and Basic Sanitation." *WHO*

40. "The Space Race." *History.com*. A&E Television Networks. 2014

41. "Catholic News, Commentary, Information, Resources, and the Liturgical Year." - *Catholic Culture*